"In reviewing *Transformed by Truth*, I was struck with the thought that God must be very pleased with the leadership of Joseph Tkach and the Worldwide Church of God team. Their courage to bring the full truth of Scripture as an illumination on long-established, misguided teaching, as well as their eagerness to join the greater Christian community as full kingdom partners, is a story that will inspire and motivate many of us who have settled into a 'comfortable' obedience to Christ."

RICHARD E. FELIX, PH.D.
PRESIDENT, AZUSA PACIFIC UNIVERSITY

"Wow! What a story! *Transformed by Truth* was a healing balm for this old preacher's cynicism. Read this book and rejoice with the angels. You'll be glad you did."

STEVE BROWN
PROFESSOR OF PREACHING AT REFORMED THEOLOGICAL SEMINARY
ORLANDO, FL

"It is with highest admiration and deepest respect that I recommend Joseph Tkach's *Transformed by Truth*. He is a man whom I consider both a brother and a friend. His transparent awakening will be a flagship for honest Truth-seekers."

WILLIAM G. BRAFFORD JR.
PASTOR, VALLEY COMMUNITY CHURCH
EL MONTE, CA

"The transformation of the Worldwide Church of God movement is a remarkable story. Every Christian should read this wonderful account of the Lord's power and grace."

DR. PAUL A. CEDAR
CHAIRMAN, MISSION AMERICA

"What rejoicing there must have been in heaven when the Worldwide Church of God repented, confirmed, and moved toward orthodoxy. I believe the story told in this important book is indeed the religious story of this decade."

DOUG ROSS
PRESIDENT, EVANGELICAL CHRISTIAN PUBLISHERS ASSOCIATION

"To know the story of these dear brothers who have truly 'tasted grace' is to be *more* than fully assured of the validity of God's miracle wrought in the Worldwide Church of God. Even more significant is to have your own heart stirred with a deeper hunger to keep that childlike humility that we *all* need if we want to *live* in grace as well as believe in it—for all our lives!"

JACK W. HAYFORD
PASTOR, THE CHURCH ON THE WAY
VAN NUYS, CA

"*Transformed by Truth* was like hearing a new Christian give his testimony. It records how a whole denomination changed from cult to mainstream because a few men were willing to follow truth, regardless of the consequences! This book will inspire all who read it. I hope other cultic denominations will follow the example of the Worldwide Church of God and let truth and grace do their sovereign work."

DALE RATZLAFF
AUTHOR OF *SABBATH IN CRISIS*
AND *THE CULTIC DOCTRINE OF SEVENTH-DAY ADVENTISTS*

"A landmark book that narrates a truly historic event. It's a gripping story that challenges Christians of all denominations to examine their beliefs and practices with openness and honesty."

DR. RUTH TUCKER
VISITING PROFESSOR, TRINITY EVANGELICAL DIVINITY SCHOOL
DEERFIELD, IL

"The apostle Paul commanded orthodox believers to be gracious in receiving 'him that is weak in the faith, but not to doubtful disputations.' I believe that the Worldwide Church of God is entitled to be accorded the opportunity to prove that it has renounced heretical doctrine and embraced the teachings of evangelical Christianity, as set forth in this book.

"The changes that have already occurred within the Worldwide Church of God are more intensive than those that brought about the Protestant Reformation. Though there are still some problems to be dealt with (as would be expected) I, for one, am extraordinarily encouraged by the reformation taking place."

DR. D. JAMES KENNEDY
SENIOR MINISTER, CORAL RIDGE PRESBYTERIAN CHURCH
FT. LAUDERDALE, FL

"This is a historic testimony of the grace of God at work in the hearts of humble Christ-followers. In this work, Joe Tkach not only chronicles the journey of the Worldwide Church of God in renewal but, most importantly, helps us all to draw defining lines between principles of the kingdom of God and human tendencies toward legalistic control and imposition. The transparency with which Joe communicates this journey is a poignant reminder that the body of Christ is built on authentic vulnerability in the community of faith."

DR. KEVIN W. MANNOIA
BISHOP, FREE METHODIST CHURCH OF NORTH AMERICA

"Picture the radical story of Paul's transformation from Judaism to Christianity. Replace that image with the Worldwide Church of God, which has experienced the supernatural and dramatic conversion from a gospel that included works, to the true gospel, which is totally based on the grace of God. You now have the picture of one of the most dramatic works of God in our century: the Worldwide Church of God, under the leadership of Joseph Tkach, transformed from human cultic teaching to the supernatural gospel of truth. This candid, behind-the-scenes account is a compelling, convicting, and awesome story of God's power."

DR. GORDON E. KIRK
SENIOR PASTOR, LAKE AVENUE CONGREGATIONAL CHURCH
PASADENA, CA

TRANSFORMED BY
TRUTH

JOSEPH TKACH

Multnomah Books *Sisters, Oregon*

TRANSFORMED BY TRUTH

published by Multnomah Publishers, Inc.

© 1997 by Joseph Tkach

International Standard Book Number: 1-57673-181-2

Printed in the United States of America

Cover photo illustration by Scott Ferguson/Ferguson & Katzman

Unless otherwise noted, Scripture quotations are from:
The Holy Bible, New International Version (NIV) © 1973, 1984 by International Bible Society,
used by permission of Zondervan Publishing House.

Also quoted:

The King James Version (KJV)

For information:
MULTNOMAH PUBLISHERS, INC.•POST OFFICE BOX 1720•SISTERS, OREGON 97759

Library of Congress Cataloging–in–Publication Data

Tkach, Joseph
    Transformed by truth/by Joseph Tkach.
        p.   cm.
    Includes index.
    ISBN 1-57673-181-2 (alk. paper)
    1. Worldwide Church of God–Doctrines–History–20th century.   2. Adventists–Doctrines–History–
20th century.   3. Sabbatarians–Doctrines–History–20th century.   4. Anglo-Israelism–History–20th
century. 5. Armstrong, Herbert W.   6. Tkach, Joseph, 1927- .   7. Tkach, Joseph.   8. Church contro-
versies–Worldwide Church of God.   9. Evangelicalism–United States–History–20th century.   I. Title.
BX6178.T53   1997
289.9–dc21   97-17764
                                                                                                    CIP

97 98 99 00 01 02 03 — 10 9 8 7 6 5 4 3 2 1

CONTENTS

FOREWORD

The Worldwide Church of God has embarked upon a course virtually uncharted in church history—a course that has taken them from the kingdom of the cults to the kingdom of Christ. In *Transformed by Truth,* Joseph Tkach, leader of the Worldwide Church of God, candidly describes the movement's transformation from the perspective of his own personal awakening. During their pilgrimage from cultism to the cross, I have come to know Joseph as both a friend and as a brother in Christ. I have observed firsthand his courage, his integrity, and his absolute commitment to Scripture as the final court of arbitration.

Joseph's personal transformation, as well as the transformation of the Worldwide Church of God, has not come without cost. Income has plummeted, staff have been laid off, membership has declined, churches have broken off into splinter groups, families have separated, and friendships have been severed.

The transformation, however, has been well worth the cost. The leadership of the Worldwide Church of God now champions essential Christian doctrine. Their flagship magazine, *The Plain Truth,* is now focused on the person and work of Jesus Christ rather than on sensationalistic end-time speculations. As Joseph wrote in the *Christian Research Journal,*

> Gone is our obsession with a legalistic interpretation of the Old Testament, our belief in British Israelism, and our insistence on our fellowship's exclusive relationship with God. Gone are our condemnations of medical science, the use of cosmetics, and traditional Christian celebrations such as Easter and Christmas. Gone is our long-held view of God as a "family" of multiple "spirit beings" into which humans may be born.

The changes within the Worldwide Church of God are a tremendous encouragement to those of us who labor in cult evangelism. If God can redirect entire movements by changing the hearts of their leaders, there's no telling what He may yet do through our continued faithfulness. The transformation of Joseph Tkach and the Worldwide Church of God is an enduring reminder that our mission is to reach, rather than repel.

HANK HANEGRAAFF
PRESIDENT, CHRISTIAN RESEARCH INSTITUTE

INTRODUCTION

While I love to read books, this is the first one I have attempted to write. As the president and pastor general of the Worldwide Church of God, I am writing to tell you a story of God's grace and the transformation that is taking place in our church. It is a transformation that can be characterized as moving from darkness to the light of God's truth. That's right, the Worldwide Church of God—the church, sect, cult, or whatever term is going through your mind, that was founded by Herbert W. Armstrong. We publish *The Plain Truth* and have reached out through the radio and television ministry of *The World Tomorrow*. We have branded evangelical Christians as false or worse. But, by God's grace we are changing. We are seeking God's will and wisdom for everything we teach and examining all that we do and say in the light of Scripture. We have grown and changed a lot in the last few years.

I want to tell you our story. It is a story of the power of prayer. It is a story of Christians reaching out to us as brothers and sisters in Christ. It is also a story of mistrust and suspicion. And, sadly, it is also a story of rejection and separation. Those who would not continue on the journey that God was taking us on have left. Family and lifelong friends have rejected some of us. But we have found new brothers and sisters who support us. Some have put their reputations on the line to say a good word for us.

I also want to tell you about my father. He was the successor to Herbert W. Armstrong. The providential grace of God caused Mr. Armstrong to entrust the future of the ministry to my father. My father was a courageous man who faithfully led us in studying the Scriptures to see where we were right and where we needed to change. He entrusted the leadership of our church to me when he died, and his struggle to follow God as a shepherd of His people has become mine.

I will tell you about the beliefs we examined and the changes that our study of God's Word brought. I will also write about Herbert W. Armstrong. He was a mentor to my father and me. I spent decades under his teaching. He was a skillful leader, and we would not be where we are today if it were not for him. Finally, I will also talk about our future in the Body of Christ. Our pilgrimage is not over. The lessons are not finished. Our exciting spiritual renewal continues.

The Worldwide Church of God (WCG) is a small denomination with a large name. In the course of its short history, there have been nearly half a million people who have passed through its doors as members. Even though the denomination never had an attendance larger than 150,000, nearly everyone has heard of *The Plain Truth* magazine, *The World Tomorrow* television program, or the Ambassador Performing Arts Concert Series in Pasadena, California. Many remember the name of Herbert W. Armstrong.

Virtually every cult-watching organization in the U.S., Canada, and Europe has devoted resources to criticizing the ministry and teachings of Herbert W. Armstrong and the movement that he started. He became famous for *The World Tomorrow* radio and television programs. His son, Garner Ted Armstrong, became the voice of these programs until he left the organization and started his own ministry in 1978.

Lacking any training in hermeneutics, epistemology, or apologetics, Herbert Armstrong began his media ministry in the early 1930s with a warning that the end of life as we know it was imminent. He was a gifted communicator. He and the ministers he trained focused on dates of the tribulation, the return of Christ, and Christ's millennial reign. Like other ministers of his time, he pioneered the use of radio in preaching about the kingdom of God. Unlike other preachers, he created hooks to capture people's attention that resulted in people's believing the marketing hooks with as much conviction as they believed the doctrines.

Herbert Armstrong's dynamic personality and work ethic led to the development and growth of his powerful, worldwide ministry. Unfortunately, the gospel message was subsumed under the prophetic predictions of a coming

European "beast" that was expected to take the United States and Britain into captivity.

While many have exited the Worldwide Church of God over the years, some still cling to Herbert W. Armstrong's teachings, and others have been transformed by the truth. Some are happy to continue believing errors, while others can't find closure on how they could have fallen for a conspiracy theory of church history and uninformed teachings. Some feel the current leaders of the Worldwide Church of God are courageous disciples of Christ, while others view them as demon possessed.

As you might imagine, some people look upon their experience in the Worldwide Church of God as nothing short of wonderful. Others reject totally the validity of what has happened. This is true with any organization—but not every organization claims to be the one and only true church of God. And herein lies the story.

In His sovereign mercy, God has moved to transform the Worldwide Church of God, and for some people, this is just too good to be true. For this reason, I felt it necessary to write this book to give my perspective on just such a story.

This book will give a behind-the-scenes look at what God has done to transform this denomination. It is my hope that I can reach out and provide a measure of closure to those who desire it.

I express my special gratitude to all those who have been supportive in our journey of transformation, as well as in the writing of this book. I am indebted to my wife, Tammy, and friends and family in Christ for their contribution of prayers and financial support. Most of all, we are appreciative of the grace of Jesus.

JOSEPH TKACH

Recent Events in the Worldwide Church of God

1986 1987 1988 1989 1990 1991 1992 1993 1994 1995 1996 1997

Death of H.W.A.
January 16, 1986

Mystery of the Ages
out of print
January 31, 1989

Book of Revelation Unveiled at Last
out of print
1989

Wonderful World Tomorrow
out of print
May 21, 1991

Launch of Global
Church of God
December 12, 1993

Doctrine of British
Israelism officially
renounced
July 13, 1995

WCG acknowledges
existence of Christians
in other denominations
April 26, 1994

Easter no longer
considered pagan
March 1996

Launch of Philadelphia
Church of God
December 19, 1989

Who Is the Beast?
out of print
May 21, 1991

Publication of
U.S. & Britain
discontinued
January 6, 1993

Launch of United
Church of God
May 3, 1995

Christmas no longer
considered pagan
September 1995

Death of
Joseph W. Tkach
September 23, 1995

CHAPTER ONE

Is This a Con?

Yeah, right.

Those two words fairly sum up the most common response of evangelicals when they hear that the Worldwide Church of God—the group Herbert W. Armstrong founded more than sixty years ago—has renounced its unbiblical teachings and has embraced Christian orthodoxy. Why, just a few short years ago, these skeptics point out, the WCG energetically denounced as "daughters of the whore of Babylon" all churches except itself. How could such a hostile, exclusivistic group be so radically transformed in so few years? And why should anyone believe that it really happened? It must be a con—there has to be some hidden agenda. I mean, come on! The Worldwide Church of God no longer a fringe sect but a part of the Christian mainstream?

Yeah, right.

OUT OF THE CAVE AND INTO THE LIGHT

I can't say I'm surprised at such suspicious reactions. After all, for most of its history, the Worldwide Church of God *has* insisted that it alone had The Truth. It has also insisted that all other churches were at best in error and at worst in league with the devil, that Herbert W. Armstrong was God's apostle and the Lord's chosen means of restoring vital long-lost truth to the world, and that those who chose to worship on Sunday rather than on the Saturday Sabbath had abandoned true religion in favor of vile paganism.

And that wasn't the worst of it!

It was as if we in the WCG had spent decades living in a cave, hurling big rocks—boulders, if we could lift them—at anyone who passed by our fortress. People soon learned to duck when they approached our door! We threw our stones year after year, broadcast after broadcast, article after article, perfectly content (well, maybe not so content, but we'll get to that part of the story a little later) to keep on chucking rocks at "the enemy"—that is, anyone who was not us. So naturally, when we recently emerged from our dark stronghold and said we wanted to talk, wise observers first insisted on examining our hands to see whether a missile or two might still be clutched there!

To be fair, I must say that not everyone in the WCG felt this way. Nevertheless, we have fifty years of publications that contain verbal sticks and stones aimed at "Christians falsely so called" (our historical phrase for biblical evangelicals).

As president of the Worldwide Church of God, I can understand why readers might be hesitant about accepting the changes that have taken place in our church over the past few years. You might still be nursing a bruise from one of our rocks, or perhaps someone in your family or circle of friends has been a long-time member and is still prone to hefting a chunk of granite now and again. Or maybe you're doubtful because you know that no unorthodox Christian sect in history (until now) has ever turned from its erring path to seek the way, the truth, and the life as proclaimed in the Bible and as reflected in "the faith which was once delivered unto the saints" (Jude 3, KJV).

I don't ask that you blindly accept the published reports that tell how we have joyfully embraced historical Christian orthodoxy; all I ask is that you honestly investigate "the plain truth" about *today's* Worldwide Church of God. As you read about the unprecedented changes that have occurred among us in the past several years, I urge you to keep an open mind about the possibility that a sovereign, omnipotent God really can take an erring church and bring it into the dazzling glories of His grace-filled truth.

I make a similar plea to WCG members who may be puzzled about the recent changes, to former members who are angry about the changes, and to members of other churches who, for one reason or another, have watched with keen interest as our drama has unfolded. No matter what your personal interest in this story may be, my goal in writing is the same: to chronicle the amazing grace of God as He sovereignly works in His church to glorify Himself and bless His people.

Even if it's hard to believe!

A FRIENDLY SKEPTIC

I won't fault any of my readers for questioning whether the changes in the WCG are real, because I recognize that even well-known Christian leaders who enthusiastically welcome our changes have sometimes wondered about their authenticity.

The Rev. D. James Kennedy is the gifted pastor of Coral Ridge Presbyterian Church in Ft. Lauderdale, Florida. Thousands know him better as the author of the witnessing tool *Evangelism Explosion*. When the changes taking place in the WCG started making headlines in evangelical publications, Dr. Kennedy was among the first to broadcast the good news through his nationwide radio program. He told his audience, "I never thought I'd be saying this, but you folks who have left the Worldwide Church of God need to go back." Soon after we learned of his encouraging comments, we made an appointment to see him at his Florida offices. We wanted to thank him and give him additional details firsthand.

On the day of our visit, four of us—Greg Albrecht, executive director of Plain Truth Ministries; Mike Feazell, church administration director; Tom Lapacka, church relations director; and I—were ushered into Dr. Kennedy's office and asked to take a seat in front of his large desk. Dr. Kennedy sat behind his desk and asked us in his deep, resonant voice, "Well, gentlemen, what can I do for you today?"

What could he do for us today? What did he mean by that? Surely he remembered why we had come—but his reserved, cautious manner suggested otherwise. I joked a bit about our visit and then thanked him for his comments on the radio. We engaged in some small talk and then began discussing the changes that had been transforming our church. He nodded politely and replied slowly from the depths of his chair, "Well, that's great. It's good you're doing this." His words said one thing, but his body language seemed to convey something quite different. It appeared that he harbored some serious skepticism about the reality of our changes. Suddenly it was almost as if the gavel came down and the bailiff called the room to order. The *Evangelism Explosion* man wanted to make sure just who was appearing in his court.

"Joe?" he asked me.

"Yes?" I replied.

"If I were Jesus Christ and you were standing before me today and I were to ask you why I should let you into My kingdom," he intoned, "what would you say?"

"That Christ's righteousness is imputed to me," I replied. I thought a direct question called for a direct answer. His face lit up like fireworks on the Fourth of July. Suddenly he was sitting bolt upright in his chair.

Quickly turning his gaze toward my associates, he asked, "And Greg? If you died today and were standing before Jesus and He asked you, 'Why should I let you into My kingdom of heaven?' what would you say?"

"By grace and through faith, by nothing I've ever done," Greg replied—an answer that got Dr. Kennedy sitting on the edge of his chair, leaning toward us.

"Well...Mike? How would you answer that question?"

By the time Mike finished and Tom was on the hot seat, Dr. Kennedy had almost leaped over his desk. His posture told the whole story. He went from sitting back in his chair—almost like a judge draped in his somber robes—to sitting on the edge of his seat, to nearly falling out of his chair. We almost wondered if he was going to hurdle his desk. By the time he had asked each of us his crucial question, he was standing up and leaning against the side of his desk, a broad smile framing the words, "All right, then!"

When he was satisfied with our answers, he picked up his phone, dialed an internal number, and said to someone on the other end, "Can we tape a radio program on this right now?" In the next few moments he made several excited calls, intending to usher us immediately into the studio. But in a few moments a staffer called to remind him that another taping session already had been scheduled—with a visitor flown in all the way from Bulgaria. In fact, the man was even then waiting patiently in the studio.

"Oh, this is terrible," Dr. Kennedy said. "Can you come back?"

Of course we agreed to return on a more suitable day. We were eager to get the word out as far as possible, because we knew from encounters just like this one that not everyone was convinced the changes rocking the WCG were genuine. Certainly Lorri McGregor had her doubts.

THAT'S WONDERFUL…IF IT'S TRUE

Lorri McGregor and her husband run a cult-watching ministry in British Columbia. Their ministry had been watchdogging us for several years, paying close attention to our published materials. She had heard about our recent changes but, like many others, wasn't so sure that any of them were authentic. One day she sent us a list of about thirty questions and inquired whether it might be possible to get together with us to hear our answers. We sent a written reply and later set up a time to meet in person. The lunch that we scheduled lasted all afternoon. Lorri had a lot of questions.

"Do you believe you're saved by grace alone?" she asked us. When we assured her we did, she responded, "Well, if you really believe that, that's just great." *If we really believe that?* Hmmm. But no time for reading between the lines; Question 2 immediately followed.

"What do you say about heaven?" she wanted to know. She knew, of course, that in the past we had taught that the unregenerate would ultimately be annihilated and that the idea of Christians going to heaven was a false doctrine. For years we had taken great glee in skewering a cartoon caricature of heaven. How ridiculous, we'd say, that the redeemed would merely sit on clouds and play harps (as if any Christian really believed that). We confessed to Lorri that we had set up a straw man and pulled it down but that now we understood from Scripture that heaven is a spiritual reality, not some physical location. When we finished answering, Lorri replied, "That's great! If that's true, then we're in agreement."

Again the "If that's true"? What's going on here?

This skeptical pattern was repeated numerous times. She would follow every one of our responses with some version of "If that's what you really believe…, If that's what you genuinely hold…, If that's true…, If that's really the way you look at it…"

After a half-dozen or so of these suspicious replies and more than an hour of conversation, I was growing a little frustrated. All of us were getting the sense that she didn't believe we were telling the truth but instead were saying only what she wanted to hear. Eventually I stopped the questioning and asked why she kept adding this maddening little rejoinder.

"Tell me, do you believe in 'justified lying'?" she asked. "Do you believe you can legitimately lie to someone who is not an authentic believer?"

"Certainly not," Mike Feazell replied. "We were far too self-righteous for that!"

And suddenly she warmed up to us.

Lorri explained that she had to ask the question about "justified lying" because she is a former Jehovah's Witness, and members of that group reportedly sometimes engage in the practice. ("Justified lying" assumes that nonbelievers do not deserve the truth, and therefore believers can lie to "outsiders" if it serves the purposes of the group.) Once Lorri understood how legalistic our church had been through the years, it made sense to her that justified lying would never have been accepted, let alone encouraged, among us. We had a truckload of problems, but justified lying wasn't among them!

In many ways, Lorri's skepticism is typical of those who continue to harbor serious doubts about the authenticity of the recent changes in the WCG. To many who knew of the church in the heyday of Herbert W. Armstrong, the changes simply appear impossible. That's not hard to understand.

THE LEFT FOOT OF EXCLUSION

Some cult watchers, ministries, churches, and pastors can be more of a hindrance when it comes to helping individuals or aberrant groups break away from their cultic theology and practice. One of our greatest challenges has been trying to explain these doctrinal reforms to outsiders while maintaining our credibility internally, and some groups have greatly hindered our efforts by their reporting.

Rumors seemed to hatch daily as we wrestled with changing our unbiblical beliefs. When some of our members noted the first changes we made, they said, "You watch! In two years they're going to be believing the Trinity and saying that Saturday isn't important anymore." Of course, none of us in leadership had any of that in mind even six years ago. So we would reply, "Sorry that you people feel this way, but we're not even thinking about the Sabbath; we're talking about the nature of God." The church in those days was such a rumor-rich environment that if I checked out a certain book from the library, it soon would be rumored that our next change would mimic the teaching of that book. We ended up saying, "Sorry, these rumors are crazy." Yet two years would go by, and we'd find ourselves looking at one of those very items our critics had predicted.

Some groups would talk to our ex-members, including those who didn't like the changes and therefore had an axe to grind. They would believe and report something that either would be a year ahead of what we were saying—thus damaging our internal credibility—or they would report that we hadn't made a certain change yet, when in fact we had—thus damaging our external credibility. Our credibility was eroded both with our own constituency and with our new evangelical friends.

One of these stories concerned a former WCG pastor. A group reported that this man left us because we were still a cult. What the report neglected to say was that the man departed while claiming to be one of the two witnesses of Revelation 11. It also did not include the fact that WCG headquarters had discovered that this man had been scamming his congregation for about four years, declaring falsely that his wife had terrible cancer. Yet the report appeared to take his side against ours, while we were trying to make major reforms in our church.

YOU'RE ON PROBATION, "BROTHER"

It's been a challenge for us to be accepted by certain evangelical or fundamental-ist groups. While we have been grateful to find that most of the Christian world rejoices in what God has done here, we also have met those who have declared openly their doubts about the authenticity of our changes. We feel much like (I suppose) Chuck Colson felt shortly after he was converted. Subsequent to being released from prison for his involvement in Watergate, Colson was watched intently by many people who couldn't believe his conversion was real. Some did not accept it for more than ten years.

A few people have told us, in essence, "Well, we're glad to hear about your supposed changes. But know this: You'll be on probation. We'll watch to see if you revert to what you were before."

That's certainly their prerogative, but our question is this: In the meantime, what are we supposed to do? Will they refuse to give us the right hand of fel-lowship until a decade or two has passed?

We understand their reluctance to accept us. We know our own history, and we know what we have historically said about believers we termed "falsely so-called Christians."

Reactions like these have made our journey a little harder. A few of our more fundamentalist brethren have been downright harsh. Ironically (because of our own heritage), it seems that the more legalistic and uptight certain groups and people seem to be, the more hesitant and guarded they are toward us.

We have wrestled with the mistrust we have met, but it has been a necessary part of our journey. We are changing at the very core of our church, and we know that changes this radical challenge the image the evangelical world has of us. We will continue our pilgrimage, and we will earn their trust.

CHAPTER TWO

CHRISTMAS EVE SERMON, 1994

No one would deny that the gospel, the message of salvation through faith in Jesus Christ, is the center of Christianity. But, it seems that Christians often get sidetracked. Unique doctrines, legalistic regulations, prophetic speculations, and personality cults seem to blur the central truths of the faith until some Christians act as if they are in a theological fog. God's light doesn't seem to be getting through the barriers they have erected.

God graciously brings renewal among His people that refocuses them on Jesus, the Author and Finisher of our faith. Faith in Christ should always be our focus. As the leaders of the WCG began to refocus the church on Christ, many members of our church doubted the changes. They thought all would soon return to the familiar ways of the past. The changes weren't for real. Talk of change must be exaggerated. Things would get back to normal.

That all changed with a landmark sermon my dad gave on Christmas Eve 1994. This is often called "The New Covenant/Old Covenant" sermon, and it once and for all convinced the skeptics within our own church that the changes were for real and that they were permanent. In that sermon, my dad demonstrated such an obvious personal conviction about salvation by grace through faith that there could no longer be any question that he was behind the changes being made. He told the membership that we were no longer going to say that those who had to work on Saturday and couldn't go to church that week were condemned to the lake of fire. He said that we were no longer going to teach triple tithing. He said so many astonishing things in his sermon that many of our older members—people who didn't believe what was happening, who dismissed what was being written in *The Plain Truth* and in the member letters and in the ministerial letters, who turned a deaf ear to what my dad was saying on video-tapes—could no longer maintain that the changes were part of a big conspiracy taking place behind my dad's back. No, it was clear there was no conspiracy and that he was intimately involved.

As a result of that sermon, the largest of three main splinter groups broke off from us and began its own organization, the United Church of God. Even though some of their leaders had been planning a breakaway in secret meetings, the sermon gave them the catalyst they needed to make their break.

Until that Christmas Eve, a lot of our own people didn't believe that the changes were real. After the sermon, however, there could be no doubt. We would pay the price.

On Christmas Eve 1994, my dad began the three-hour sermon by saying, "This is going to be a long afternoon." His message would fundamentally change forever the Worldwide Church of God. As one writer later put it, my dad "had to show that it is not a sin to work on the Sabbath. This was *the* single most important decision in the history of the denomination.[1]

My father knew he might touch off a firestorm with this sermon. Toward the end of his message he said: "Some people will rejoice about what I have said today, some will criticize. But I can't let the potential for criticism prevent me from preaching and teaching about the New Covenant and new understanding we have in Jesus Christ." Because my dad was dedicated to faithfully serving Jesus Christ by leading our church into truth, he plowed ahead. He gave this sermon several times in various locations around the country to maximize its impact and to minimize misunderstanding. In three hours he covered a wide assortment of topics. In some of his most important remarks he:

- affirmed that the church is no longer bound to the Old Covenant but is in fact a New Covenant organism;
- insisted that salvation is by grace through faith and is not gained in the least through law keeping;
- declared that members who needed to work on Saturday to care for their families were not committing sin;
- proclaimed that tithing is not a requirement for salvation but is a voluntary action performed in service and love to God

In many ways an observer cannot grasp the importance of the sermon without reading it in its entirety. Yet how many readers would be willing to sift through sixty-two single-spaced pages of sermon transcripts? Allow me to reproduce just a few highlights from the message. I hope the reader appreciates that the excerpts that follow were spoken and are reproduced from the audio/video transcripts we have on file. These should be sufficient to gain an appreciation for the incalculable impact the sermon had on our church:

We were all in darkness and dungeons and blind and illiterate when it comes to understanding the plan for salvation. He, Christ, is the life for both Jews and Gentiles. He opens the eyes of the spiritually blind. And he brings freedom to those who have been enslaved by sin. And he is the covenant that God makes with His people. He is the basis for our relationship with God.... It is only through Him that we can receive promises of the new covenant....

We let our light shine so that our Father in heaven is glorified, He is worshiped, He is praised, and He is thanked.... Before it was, more or less, pray and pay. Don't worry about anything else. All you were required to do was to send your tithes in, read the literature, and shut up. It goes beyond that....

Salvation is a gift, and it means that you cannot earn it in any way, shape, or form. And that was one of the major discussions that came from my relationship with Mr. Armstrong.... I began to explain what a new convert would have to go through before he was just invited to attend church for the first time. It was like going through an inquisition. Given the third degree. And you know, maybe it was sincere on the part of the ministry. But also they were doing what they were informed to do from headquarters. Mr. Armstrong said that was not his [intent]. And he went on to prove [it] to me. He said, "I baptized people who were still smoking. I baptized drunkards. I baptized, you know, everything you could think of. Even teenagers." He said, "In other words, you're saying that we were expecting people to perform and act like Christians before they could become a Christian?" I said, "I guess that's it." He said, "That's the reason why I baptized these people, so that they would receive God's Spirit and with it they would have the conviction and they would have the desire and inspiration to accomplish, to overcome some of those physical handicaps that we have...."

We are justified by faith. We are declared right with God by faith. We are saved on the basis of faith. Not on law keeping....

And he [Mr. Armstrong] brought up another interesting point. Especially the comment when he said that there are Christians elsewhere in the world. "Oh, but if they don't have the Sabbath as a sign, how can they be Christians?" Well, we don't have the Sabbath as a sign, either. Does that mean I am minimizing the importance of the Sabbath? Absolutely not. Our sign is faith in Jesus Christ, and as a result we are baptized and receive the Holy Spirit....

When judgment day comes and the judge asks us why He should let us into His kingdom, how do you think we're going to answer? "Oh, I have a perfect Sabbath attendance record. I have kept all of the laws flawlessly." You say that, you made one big blunder, because you didn't. And He will be quick to point it out to you. "I've interceded for you every day, you dummy." I hope we don't do that, because the judge could easily point out laws we haven't [kept]. Where we have failed and sins that we have committed. And in some cases, not even repented of. We can't say that we're good enough to keep the law. All we can do is plead for mercy. I want that, I want that. We have faith in Christ that He died to redeem us from all sins. He died to rescue us from the penalty of the law, and that's our only basis for salvation....

James, like Paul, warns us about a so-called faith that does not lead to obeying God. Paul is talking about real faith. The kind that includes repentance, total allegiance to Christ. A wholehearted willingness to obey Him. But even then he says, it is the faith that saves us and not the works. But we have works because we are saved....

That's the spirit and the attitude of a real Christian. Not those that want to dig in their heels and say, "I don't agree with it!" Well, you can do that with the Global Church of God if you want. If you want to go back to legalism, fine! I would wish that you wouldn't. But if that's the only way you need to learn—get your nose really rubbed into it—and you've not learned enough about legalism that you want to put it out of your life, well then, go ahead....

So under the New Covenant the tithe is voluntary—done out of love and allegiance to Jesus Christ, and isn't that appropriate? Shouldn't our giving be done out of the vision, the love of God in our hearts? That's the way; that's what separates the men from the boys....

Sometimes it seems as if the Sabbath was more important than human lives. Or the Sabbath was more important than expressing love and faith in Christ. We looked at the external instead of the internal. We meant well. But now we can change because God has led us to a deeper understanding of the covenant....

The Sabbath was the sign of the Old Covenant with Israel. Faith in

Christ and the Spirit of God (if you are looking for a sign) is the sign between the servants of God today. It is not the sign of the New Covenant of the blood of Christ. The sign of the New Covenant is faith in Christ and the bread and wine, which are symbols of that covenant. Consequently, the Sabbath to be observed under the New Covenant differs from the way it was to be observed under the Old. The Lord of the Sabbath has come, and the reality has replaced the shadow. Colossians 3:17, the New Testament Sabbath. The Sabbath rest that remains for the people of God in Hebrews 4 is a new life in Christ. The life of faith in Him and the light of the Spirit. The way we observed the Sabbath in the past has been to apply the Old Covenant rules to the New Covenant Sabbath. Like oil and water. And thereby applying unnecessary burdens which, like I said earlier, the ministry did not have to experience....

No one is trying to water down the law of God or what God commands and expects of us. I've always said, we go above and beyond the call of duty. But we don't impose hardships on people that God didn't. Are we more righteous than God? Are we like the Pharisees which Christ took to task and said that if our righteousness doesn't exceed theirs we will in no way inherit the kingdom of God?...

We should all welcome each other based on faith in Christ. That's the important issue. The point is that we should not be sitting in judgment on others and how they observe the Sabbath. Some will be extra careful to be home by sundown [on Friday], while others will not....

The Sabbath is a shadow pointing us to the reality, who is Christ. That doesn't mean that the Sabbath is done away with, but it means the Sabbath is fulfilled in Christ. It means that Christ is more important than the Sabbath. The Sabbath rest for Christians in Hebrews 4 is the new life in Christ. Not just a day of the week. And Paul tells us in Romans 14 that we should not be involved in arguments or disputes over days. Being Sabbath keepers does not make us more righteous than other Christians.

God respects our willingness to sacrifice to obey Him even though our understanding was incomplete. God doesn't hold it against us. But now God has called on the church to grow deeper in understanding. To worship Christ and not the Sabbath. The Sabbath was not made to be worshiped; Christ is to be worshiped....

When he finally began wrapping up his sermon three hours after he began, my dad reminded his listeners once more: "We are saved by faith, not by rules—and certainly not by judging one another. And I am sure this is going to cause a lot of questions, and that's good. It shows you are thinking. And hopefully it is with a positive spirit and a positive attitude. I encourage you to study this topic.... I ask you to pray daily for [Christ] to continue to guide us into more truth and more understanding. I thank you for your loyalty and I thank you for your support and cooperation." He declared he had simply done his best to make clear what God was teaching him and once more asked for rumors to be kept under control, "even though it will be a challenge, I'm sure."

Boy, did he hit that one on the head.

The sermon was a turning point in the renewal of our church. We had begun examining our teachings and had made some changes. When my father made it clear that legalistic interpretations of Old Covenant regulations were not going to be the central focus of our ministry, he cleared away the fog that was clouding our view of Jesus Christ. The pilgrimage continued for me and for our church. We continued coming out of a theological sleep into the refreshing light of a clear focus on the gospel of grace and our relationship with our Savior, Jesus Christ.

CHAPTER THREE

MY PILGRIMAGE

Several years ago the famous neurologist Dr. Oliver Sacks wrote a fascinating book titled *Awakenings*. His book, which later inspired a movie starring Robin Williams, told the remarkable stories of several long-term coma patients who were finally (but not always permanently) coaxed out of their deep slumber by doctors using unorthodox methods. The book is both a celebration of human consciousness and a profound meditation on the mystery of life.

Dr. Sacks's book suggests a useful metaphor for describing what has happened to us in the Worldwide Church of God over the past few years. By the grace of God, we have awakened out of our deep theological slumber. No longer does our faith consist primarily of a grab bag of esoteric doctrines. Today we enjoy and are actively exploring a personal relationship with our living Savior, Jesus Christ.

One biblical text especially comes to mind when I think of our recent spiritual awakening. John 5 ministers powerfully to me, but I am particularly drawn to the end of the chapter where Jesus says to the Jews, "You diligently study the Scriptures because you think that by them you possess eternal life. These are the Scriptures that testify about me, yet you refuse to come to me to have life" (John 5:39–40).

For so many long years, this is exactly the error we made! We searched the

Scriptures diligently to discover the right twist to this doctrine or the correct slant to that one. We got lost in minutiae and largely missed the real treasure, Jesus Christ Himself. We didn't completely ignore Jesus, but to us He was little more than a messenger, a newscaster of prophesied events, and a man who somehow lived a life free of sin. We searched the Scriptures because in them we thought we had eternal life; yet we did not come fully to Jesus that we might truly live.

This passage in John, as well as the rest of the gospel, has been a tremendous, eye-opening blessing to us. Why? It trumpets the deity of Christ and celebrates who He claims to be. Its simple proclamation has been a powerful help to us, as have John's epistles. Can you imagine what it is like to be greeted by such an overwhelmingly attractive Presence upon awaking from a decades-long slumber? It is nothing short of miraculous.

WHEN DID YOU COME TO THE LORD?

Since the news about our changes in the WCG began to spread in the evangelical world, Greg Albrecht, Mike Feazell, and I (and others) have periodically been asked to appear on various Christian radio and television programs. Inevitably the host will ask us, "When did you come to the Lord?" A good portion of these folks seem to want us to name a particular point in time when we entered the kingdom of God. Others are content simply to know that we did so, even if we can't name the day and the hour of our conversion. They don't push for a specific answer or insist that if we can't name a particular day and hour our experience is invalid.

Frankly, this question of when we came to know the Lord presents a problem for us. Long before the changes began, all of us were functioning as ministers. We were baptizing people and performing weddings and counseling and preaching sermons years before the transformation of our church. So what should we say about our ministry before the changes took place? Was it invalid? Was it un-Christian? Was it illegitimate? Do we believe that the only true ministry we've performed occurred after the changes and not a moment before?

I don't think so. For a number of us, this waking out of sleep has been a slow, yet steady process. It's been progressive, not sudden. Over a number of years we began to come to the Lord and understand what it meant to have a personal relationship with Him. God has led us gently; Jesus as our Shepherd has been patient. I don't believe our story in this regard is unique; the widely respected and best-selling evangelical author Philip Yancey says something about this in his award-winning book, *The Jesus I Never Knew.* At the outset of his literary journey to understand the Jesus of the Gospels, Yancey confesses that his grasp of the Savior has changed greatly over the years:

> Jesus, I found, bore little resemblance to the Mister Rogers figure I had met in Sunday School, and was remarkably unlike the person I had studied in Bible college. For one thing, he was far less tame. In my prior image, I realized, Jesus' personality matched that of a *Star Trek* Vulcan: he remained calm, cool, and collected as he strode like a robot among excitable human beings on spaceship earth. That is not what I found portrayed in the Gospels and in the better films. Other people affected Jesus deeply: obstinacy frustrated him, self-righteousness infuriated him, simple faith thrilled him. Indeed, he seemed more emotional and spontaneous than the average person, not less. More passionate, not less...
>
> Sometimes I have felt like a tourist walking around a great monument, awed and overwhelmed. I circle the monument of Jesus, inspecting its constituent parts—the birth stories, the teachings, the miracles, the enemies and followers—in order to reflect on and try to comprehend the man who has changed history.
>
> Other times I have felt like an art restorer stretched out on the scaffolding of the Sistine Chapel, swabbing away the grime of history with a moistened Q-tip. If I scrub hard enough, will I find the original beneath all those layers?[1]

Our own understanding of and appreciation for the Master also has changed over the years, although I'm certain our perceptions have changed more radically than Yancey's! Still, in many places where Yancey's book articulates how his views changed, his experience mirrors our own. We did not one morning suddenly turn around and bump into the real Jesus; it's more like we had been shadowing Him from a distance for a long time, and only recently did we get close enough to glimpse His face.

A KINSHIP WITH PETER

In my personal testimony I sometimes compare my spiritual experience to that of the apostle Peter. Before Christ is crucified, Peter is with Him, eating, living, and interacting with Him for at least three years. Yet at crunch time, Peter vigorously denies his Lord three times. Along with all the other disciples, he flees into the night, leaving Jesus to face the cross alone. Three days later Christ conquers death and rises from the grave. One of His first actions is to bring Peter back into the fold. Then Pentecost comes and we see a different Peter—now he's preaching in the faces of the Sanhedrin; now he's giving his first sermon and three thousand people are convicted and converted; now he's the unquestioned human leader of the fledgling church.

Here's the problem: If you had to identify the time when Peter was converted, what would you say? Was he a believer when Jesus told him, "Get behind me, Satan!" (Matthew 16:23)? Was he a believer when he three times denied the Lord? Did he become a believer after he was convinced of the resurrection? Or did he enter the kingdom at Pentecost when the Holy Spirit was poured out on the church? I'm not sure. The one thing I am sure of, however, is that the Peter I see in Acts is *definitely* a believer—and a bold and uncompromising one at that.

When I consider Peter in both his before and after versions, I find it natural to identify with him. No doubt I've grown tremendously in my understanding of the faith in these past few years, but I firmly believe I was a convert to Christ long before that.

THE CLEANEST FEELING I'VE EVER KNOWN

I can't say for sure the exact moment I was converted. I do know I experienced the cleanest feeling I've ever enjoyed in my life in 1971 when I was baptized. I felt that I was born again (even though I was told I was only conceived). I had an experience that was remarkable, genuine, and true.

Perhaps this will mean more to you if you understand something about what our church culture was like a few decades ago. I regretfully admit that the experience of Ambassador College for some people more closely resembled an indoctrination camp than it did an undergraduate institution of higher learning. Many students felt a covert pressure (at least in the sixties and seventies) to be baptized by the end of their freshman year. If you didn't get baptized by the end of your first year, some assumed that you simply weren't mature and that probably something was very wrong in your spiritual life. If you entered your sophomore year as an unbaptized student, the peer pressure really mounted. Only rarely did people make it past their second year without succumbing to the pressure. If you were an upperclassman and not be baptized, you had to be a real rebel.

All but two in my class were baptized their freshman year; I was one of the "unwashed." Other students came up to the two of us and said things like, "You know, I've just got to tell you, I'm really kind of perplexed at what I see. Why aren't you baptized? What's wrong with you?" I remember clearly the concerns I had. I could see that some of my friends were baptized, but their behavior and conduct seemed to be the same or even worse than before they had made this commitment. I knew I was no one to judge, but I didn't want that to be my story too. I wanted to get baptized at some point, but I was genuinely disturbed by what I saw…and I let people know about it.

My views were not warmly received.

Still I waited. I wanted to be sure that I was doing the right thing; I wanted to be certain I knew what I was doing. To me, baptism was very serious. I finally took the plunge, so to speak, in my junior year. When I slid under the waters of baptism, I knew that all my sins had been forgiven. I felt tremendously good about that. I didn't want to commit another sin from that point on! It took only a day to crush my naive hope. All these girls were coming up and hugging me, and I couldn't help but think, *Wow! Now I see why my buddies are getting baptized!*

I don't mean to suggest that my baptism is what saved me; no mere ritual can do that. Since I already have mentioned the kinship I feel with Peter, perhaps it would be appropriate here to quote him on the significance of baptism. His words well summarize what I was feeling that day:

> This water symbolizes baptism that now saves you also—not the removal of dirt from the body but the pledge of a good conscience toward God. It saves you by the resurrection of Jesus Christ, who has gone into heaven and is at God's right hand—with angels, authorities and powers in submission to him. (1 Peter 3:21–22)

By the time I was baptized, I already had a saving relationship with Jesus Christ—even though it was encrusted with layer upon layer of theological barnacles. When those barnacles finally started coming off a few years ago, what a massive weight was dropped into the depths of the ocean! I had not known what I was missing for so long. My eyes—our eyes—at last were being opened, and we were emerging from a deep, deep sleep.

HALLMARKS OF THE AWAKENING

Some people might expect that when God began to rouse us from our theological slumber, He would wake us up with mighty demonstrations of power and extraordinary signs and wonders. But that's not how He worked His miracle with us. We had long held a negative view of charismatic manifestations, so perhaps it's not surprising that Jesus would not lead us toward those things in our fellowship; we've always been a bit more Presbyterian or Anglican in our worship. Would God have led a lot of people in our fellowship at this crucial time to some sort of awakening that highlighted all kinds of charismatic gifts? I doubt it. We wouldn't have known what to do with it. For good reason, I think, the move of the Holy Spirit through our fellowship has been cautious and progressive.

Nevertheless, we can point to several hallmarks that powerfully indicate just how greatly God has transformed us. These things are both past and ongoing and show that something dramatic has happened over a short period of time in our church. We were in darkness; now we are walking in light more than ever before.

1. New comprehension of Scripture

It's easiest to sleep when you're in the dark. That's true in both the physical and the spiritual realms. If you want to wake someone up either from spiritual or physical sleep, flood the room with light. It may take awhile to rouse the sleeper, but eventually light wins. And then what sights there are to see!

We have found this to be delightfully true in our understanding of Scripture. I've already mentioned what a help the writings of the apostle John have been to me. Throughout his Gospel he contrasts light with darkness and how people living in the darkness can come into the light of life. At one point he quotes Jesus: "Light has come into the world, but men loved darkness instead of light because their deeds were evil. Everyone who does evil hates the light, and will not come into the light for fear that his deeds will be exposed. But whoever lives by the truth comes into the light, so that it may be seen plainly that what he has done has been done through God" (John 3:19–21).

I can point to several defining moments in my life when the light of Scripture blazed in my mind with a power and clarity I had never known before. I think of the time when Galatians 3:13–14 leaped off the page and slapped me in the face: "Christ redeemed us from the curse of the law by becoming a curse for us, for it is written: 'Cursed is everyone who is hung on a tree.' He redeemed us in order that the blessing given to Abraham might come to the Gentiles through Christ Jesus, so that by faith we might receive the promise of the Spirit." This is not a text that a lifelong legalist can safely read! Another defining moment came when I read Galatians 2:14: "When I saw that they [Peter and his friends] were not acting in line with the truth of the gospel, I said to Peter in front of them all, 'You are a Jew, yet you live like a Gentile and not like a Jew. How is it, then, that you force Gentiles to follow Jewish customs?'" Gulp! That is precisely what we had been doing for decades; we insisted that Gentiles should live like Jews. How could we have missed this?

I recall one time reading about the transfiguration, when Moses and Elijah appeared on the mountaintop with Jesus and all three blazed with an otherworldly light. Peter and the other two disciples who witnessed the event were so frightened they did not know what to say, but Peter, in typical fashion, spoke up anyway and suggested that he and his friends should build three tabernacles for Jesus and Moses and Elijah. Suddenly it struck me like never before: "Wow! Is this loaded with meaning! *He picked the two most important guys from the Old Testament.* Boy! John is talking about the law and the prophets—and you don't build tabernacles for them. *Here's* the glory—Jesus! He's not just some messenger; He *is* the message. And I missed it! Until now, I didn't see any of it."

Where was I? It was as if I were at last emerging from a massive cloud bank, an impenetrable blanket of fog that had obscured my vision my whole life. Finally I was stepping out of the darkness and into the light. At last I could see John's point!

The last three years, every time I have read the Bible I find myself exclaiming, "Wow!" It's a wonderful, exquisite feeling. It's great. And I can't help but wonder: *How did I miss it?*

2. Attitude toward Old Testament purity laws

In the past we practiced all the Old Testament laws of purity and therefore refused to eat the foods listed as unclean in Leviticus 11. Pork and shellfish and a myriad other foods were off-limits. Imagine how difficult this could be when one of us visited a restaurant with some friends. More than one of us got bug-eyed if we got a bowl of soup that might possibly contain a bit of ham; it was not unusual to ask our waitress if the refried beans contained any lard. Some of our members would get around this by eating whatever they ordered, without asking questions "for conscience' sake." They'd order, assume there might be lard in the beans, but not ask about it, and eat it anyway.

Today, members throughout our fellowship are discovering a newfound freedom as expressed in texts like Colossians 2:16–17, 20–22:

Therefore do not let anyone judge you by what you eat or drink, or with regard to a religious festival, a New Moon celebration or a Sabbath day. These are a shadow of the things that were to come; the reality, however, is found in Christ....

Since you died with Christ to the basic principles of this world, why, as though you still belonged to it, do you submit to its rules: "Do not handle! Do not taste! Do not touch!"? These are all destined to perish with use, because they are based on human commands and teachings.

A big part of our waking out of sleep is that many people have felt tremendous liberation from the bondage of the past and have expressed a need to act in certain, symbolic ways. For instance, after my dad gave his Christmas Eve sermon in 1994, some people went out immediately afterward to a lobster dinner. It wasn't that they needed lobster; they wanted to make the statement, "I'm not bound by this anymore." In some ways, they were following in the footsteps of Martin Luther several centuries before, when he broke with the medieval Catholic church and married Katherine Von Bora—something that had been forbidden to him in his life as a monk.

How times have changed! It's been fun for me to watch some of my closest associates, including Greg Albrecht and Mike Feazell, on this issue. One time, Greg and Mike and I were in a restaurant, and Mike said, "I'm going to have a pepperoni pizza. I hope this doesn't offend you. This is symbolic for me, symbolic that the church of God is bigger than us!"

Greg and I looked at each other and said, "Hey! Go for it, Mike!"

I've had lunch or dinner with several others who have ordered similar items. I don't know if they're eating these things just to see how I react or if they really want to enjoy the new experience. One friend, a longtime church member, ordered a plate of mussels. Every insect in the ocean was on his plate. And you know what? It really didn't trouble me at all.

I've tasted shrimp, I've tasted pork, I've tasted just about everything now. But because my grandmother and my dad and my aunt all died of colon cancer, and since I have a genetic predisposition to getting the same disease—I have a one in four chance—I hardly eat beef, let alone pork. I am Mr. Fiber Man. Some of my friends think that I cut out a little corner of the carpet every morning and put it in the blender. I want *fiber.*

But if the craving for pepperoni ever does strike, I can party just as hearty as my friend Mike. And God is pleased.

3. Attitude toward the Saturday Sabbath

For many years our church taught that the key sign to identifying God's true church was the keeping of the Saturday Sabbath. There is no question that some of us worshiped the day instead of worshiping God. One of our former pastors gave a series of seven sermons on how to keep the Sabbath. In one sermon he used an extreme example to illustrate his point. He asked the members of his congregation to imagine they were home on a Saturday when someone fell down in front of their home or perhaps was injured in a car accident. Suppose this injured party came to their door, cut and bleeding, and asked for help or to use the phone. What should godly WCG members tell such a person? Here's what I was told this pastor recommended: "Look, this is my Sabbath day, and I'm resting today. Could you please go next door? If there's nobody there, fine, then you can come back and I'll see how I can help you."

Believe it or not, this was seen as proper and righteous conduct by some in our fellowship. This is how they taught one should worship God. Most of us did not take things to such an extreme, but some did. They failed to see that such behavior demonstrated they were worshiping the day rather than the Lord of the day. They should have reread what Matthew wrote on the subject:

> At that time Jesus went through the grainfields on the Sabbath. His disciples were hungry and began to pick some heads of grain and eat them. When the Pharisees saw this, they said to him, "Look! Your disciples are doing what is unlawful on the Sabbath."

He answered, "Haven't you read what David did when he and his companions were hungry? He entered the house of God, and he and his companions ate the consecrated bread—which was not lawful for them to do, but only for the priests. Or haven't you read in the Law that on the Sabbath the priests in the temple desecrate the day and yet are innocent? I tell you that one greater than the temple is here. If you had known what these words mean, 'I desire mercy, not sacrifice,' you would not have condemned the innocent. For the Son of Man is Lord of the Sabbath."

Going on from that place, he went into their synagogue, and a man with a shriveled hand was there. Looking for a reason to accuse Jesus, they asked him, "Is it lawful to heal on the Sabbath?"

He said to them, "If any of you has a sheep and it falls into a pit on the Sabbath, will you not take hold of it and lift it out? How much more valuable is a man than a sheep! Therefore it is lawful to do good on the Sabbath."

Then he said to the man, "Stretch out your hand." So he stretched it out and it was completely restored, just as sound as the other. (Matthew 12:1–13)

Texts like these forced us to see that Jesus is the Lord of our lives, but the converse was true and shocking to some of our members. The Sabbath day is not the Lord of our lives. Jesus has come into our fellowship and into our individual lives and claimed His rightful lordship. This major change was part of our waking out of sleep, part of our coming to Jesus. It was an issue God forced us to deal with.

Anyone—whether he's a Saturday or Sunday Sabbatarian or whether he's bound by some other legalistic doctrine that vies for lordship of his life—is going to have to struggle through the same black hole we did. Jesus is Lord, not the day. We were so focused on the day that we felt made us special and unique that we failed to understand that Jesus is Lord of all days and of all time. We worship

Christ, not the Sabbath. Legalism blinded us from seeing what should have been so plain. And that legalism is still a plague today—not just with groups like ours, but with all of the evangelical world. It has to be identified, rooted out, and purged. The Lord of the Sabbath requires it.

4. The emergence of small groups

In the past, members of the Worldwide Church of God prayed alone, rarely in groups. We misunderstood the words of Jesus when He said: "But when you pray, go into your room, close the door and pray to your Father, who is unseen. Then your Father, who sees what is done in secret, will reward you" (Matthew 6:6). We did not understand He was using a picture to illustrate that prayer is not for show, that prayer as some of the Pharisees practiced it was empty and meant only to impress people. We took His words literally and missed His whole point. We taught that one should pray alone and that it was wrong to pray in groups.

Somehow we missed the fact that Jesus Himself often prayed in public (see Matthew 6:9–13; 11:25–26; John 11:41–42; 17). Somehow we didn't notice that the early church loved to pray in groups (see Acts 1:24–25; 4:23–31; 12:12–17; 13:3; etc.).

Here, too, God has led us out of darkness and into His brilliant light!

Today, small group fellowships are blossoming in our church. We've gone from no small groups to having over eleven hundred of them throughout our church. This is a miracle. Never before would we have prayed together. Never before would we have studied the Bible together. Never before would we have encouraged men and women to sit together while a woman read Scripture.

Now we urge our members to join accountability groups in which they pray and study and commit themselves to seeking the welfare of everyone in the group. I'm a member of a small group myself.

And the result? Our people have experienced the unity and special bond that come from praying together and studying the Scriptures together in small groups. It may not seem like a big deal to outsiders—small groups have been growing in popularity in the church for decades now—but to us, it's a major, unprecedented step into the light. It's so much fun being awake!

5. Embracing other Christians

In the old days it was common for our members to look askance at people from other denominations. We thought of them as "Christians falsely so-called," as "deceived," and even went to the extreme of regarding them as "children of the devil."

Thankfully, those days are past. Now our members are able to embrace other Christians as genuine brothers and sisters in the Lord. No longer do we regard them as deluded or fifth-column people. We are all one in Christ, and we can joyfully urge our people to "Make every effort to keep the unity of the Spirit through the bond of peace. There is one body and one Spirit—just as you were called to one hope when you were called—one Lord, one faith, one baptism; one God and Father of all, who is over all and through all and in all" (Ephesians 4:3–6).

6. Ministers joining local associations

To fully appreciate this final hallmark of the Holy Spirit's dramatic reformation of our fellowship, one has to appreciate the depth of our former exclusivity. Never before would our ministers have anything to do with pastors from other denominations. What has light to do with darkness, or Christ with Belial? The distrustful attitudes held by our members toward outsiders was multiplied many times over in our ministers.

This is beginning to change. Many of our ministers have joined the local ministerial association in their city. Our ministers have joined transdenominational prayer groups and are getting to know other pastors in their cities, meeting with them for prayer and fellowship. Our pastors and members assist in Billy Graham crusades, Promise Keepers rallies, and a host of cross-denominational evangelistic and service projects.

A lot of good things have developed out of this interchurch activity, perhaps most notably the new places of worship we have gained. With few exceptions, we rent or lease facilities for our local church services; not many of our congregations own their own property. Now, instead of meeting in Masonic lodges and bingo halls, many of our churches partner with other congregations in sanctuaries designed for worship. We use their facilities on Saturday while they use them on Sunday. Many denominations have been helpful to us in this regard, led numerically by Foursquare Gospel and Missouri Synod Lutheran churches.

For our ministers to join a local pastoral prayer group is such an incredible step forward for us. It certainly wouldn't have happened even five to seven years ago. Yet most of our pastors are seeking out such groups. This tremendous hallmark demonstrates the enormous change that has taken place in their own spiritual lives. This development alone shows how powerfully God has been at work in us in the past few years, and we are eternally grateful for His intervention.

THE NEED FOR ROMANS 14

It is wonderful to walk in the daylight after so many years spent slumbering in the darkness, but we have found that it takes awhile for our eyes to get used to the bright Sonshine. Many of what I have called hallmarks also call for a high degree of tolerance within our fellowship. Many of our people still see some of these hallmarks as sinful. We have had to cling to Romans 14 for guidance. In that chapter Paul gave so many helpful directions for dealing in a godly way with "disputable things." I'd like to quote the whole chapter, but I'll restrain myself. Permit me to recall verses 19–20: "Let us therefore make every effort to do what leads to peace and to mutual edification. Do not destroy the work of God for the sake of food. All food is clean, but it is wrong for a man to eat anything that causes someone else to stumble."

Part of waking out of sleep for us has been to understand what these verses mean. If we are to act in love, we simply can't go out and do everything that we might be justified in doing. Our brothers and sisters in Christ are more important than meat and drink, and we must remember this always—especially in view of our peculiar history.

A REAL CHALLENGE

It is a real challenge to explain these issues of liberty to some of our folks who still cling to the old order. On the one hand we've explained there's no sin in devotion; if you want to be a Sabbatarian and you do this as to the Lord, more power to to you. Great! But as soon as you say it's what someone *has* to do and you try to force your standard of righteousness on others, you've crossed the line.

I try to explain it in this way: If your devotion is in response to God's love, that's fantastic. But if you're going through these exercises to stand in His good favor, then you've missed the boat.

Some of those who struggle the most are people I know so well, such as in my extended family. I've had a few conversations about this with one of my relatives "Don't you see, Joe, that it's a means to worship God," she has told me. "Yes," I have responded, "I see it as a means to worship God. But my relationship isn't through the configuration of the sun and the moon and the earth. It's through the living Savior, Jesus Christ. He is the fulfillment of the Law, and He's the one I serve. Not the Sabbath."

Because of these challenges, tolerance on this issue has been the order of the day. "One man considers one day more sacred than another," wrote Paul, "another man considers every day alike. Each one should be fully convinced in his own mind" (Romans 14:5). If our goal is to serve and worship the Lord Jesus, then tolerance is an absolute requirement. And in our case, so is something else.

AN INDISPENSABLE SENSE OF HUMOR

I doubt we would have made it this far without a healthy sense of humor. To keep our sanity (not to mention our sanctification) we have found it necessary to make fun of ourselves and laugh at events and at each other. That's helped tremendously.

Sometime ago I received a letter from a man taking me to task because the WCG now says it's OK to celebrate Christmas. In the past this was absolutely forbidden.

"Can't you just see the problem?" he demanded. "Satan is right in Santa!"

I quickly wrote back and made several points, including this one: "It's no legitimate proof of anything, but can't you see that *God* spelled backward is *dog?*" My point, of course, was that matching up corresponding letters in two distinct words is without value. You can prove anything you want to with that sort of reasoning.

A few days later I was watching *Saturday Night Live,* and comedian Dana Carvey was doing his Church Lady character. "She" had a little board with magnetic letters spelling out "Santa." Then she said, in a conspiratorial voice, "Have you noticed something here?" Her hands moved to the board and rearranged the letters to spell *Satan.* "Could it be?" she asked, her raised eyebrows pointing skyward.

And I thought, *Mr. Carvey must know us.*

BRING ON THE SONSHINE!

We were asleep for so many years that now we revel in each waking moment. We much prefer the world of light to the world of darkness, the land of reality to the land of shadows. As the apostle Paul wrote: "Everything exposed by the light becomes visible, for it is light that makes everything visible. This is why it is said:

> Wake up, O sleeper,
> rise from the dead,
> and Christ will shine on you.
>   (Ephesians 5:13–14)

This is a great promise, and a faithful one. Take it from somebody who knows. It's good to rise from the sleep of death. And it's even better to bask in the Sonshine of the Master's boundless, red-hot love.

CHAPTER FOUR

THE RIGHT HAND
OF FELLOWSHIP

When word first started to circulate about the transformation taking place in the Worldwide Church of God, my dad received a call from Calvin Burrell, president of the Church of God (Seventh Day). This church was the parent organization of the Radio Church of God, which Herbert Armstrong founded. For sixty years we had called this church "dead," identifying it as the Church of Sardis mentioned in Revelation 3 (while we, of course, believed we were the living Church of Philadelphia). The conversation between my dad and Mr. Burrell eventually led to a meeting in Denver, Colorado, between representatives of his church and Greg Albrecht, Mike Feazell, me, and Victor Kubik (who has since left us for a splinter group).

We were not surprised to find these gentlemen were wonderful brothers. While they didn't understand or necessarily agree with everything that was happening in our church, they did welcome many of our changes. They were glad to meet with us and *very* happy when we said that we would no longer pejoratively label them "dead" and identify them with the Church of Sardis.

As we returned home from this landmark meeting, we reflected on our disintegrating exclusivity. We had long taught that the Worldwide Church of God was the only true church. This meeting showed us we were wrong.

Shortly after we met with representatives of the Church of God (Seventh

Day) we somehow came into contact with Sabbatarian Christians living in the Ukraine. To the surprise of some of our denominational leaders, these people seemed to be genuine believers. So despite our longstanding exclusivist, separatist practices, even some of our hardliners felt safe with these people because they lived in the Ukraine, a world away. They spoke Russian and therefore wouldn't be attending our church. They could be accepted as true Christians…from a safe distance. Doing so wouldn't disturb our lives of faith.

Even before this, my dad had begun to say publicly, "You know, there are Christians in other churches, whether they're keeping Saturday or Sunday." That breakthrough recognition was met with profound resistance from many quarters in the church but was the first step toward reconciliation with Christians from many denominations.

BILL BRAFFORD AND THE FOURSQUARE GOSPEL CHURCH

After we started making significant doctrinal changes in 1987, the first evangelical pastor I talked to who was cheering us on and who showed us any Christian brotherhood was Bill Brafford, the pastor of Valley Community, a Foursquare Gospel congregation in El Monte, California.

It's interesting how we met. Years ago the family of a lay elder in Bill's congregation used to attend our church. This elder, Bill Burns, even went to Imperial Schools, our high school. Bill has always been the kind of guy who might say or do anything—the kind of personality that presents real challenges for legalism.

Bill Burns ended up going to Vietnam. Sometime after he returned home, he started attending Bill Brafford's church. Whenever he heard people in his congregation say disparaging things about the Worldwide Church of God, he would reply, "Hey, don't do that! My parents used to attend there. There are a lot of good people there. A lot of knuckleheads, but a lot of good people too." Eventually this came to the attention of his pastor, who gave Bill what I consider uncommon advice. After hearing Bill's painful story of his own experiences in the WCG, his pastor told him: "You still have some issues you need to reconcile over there. You ought to go over to the Worldwide Church of God and talk to those folks.

Go there, unburden yourself, and rectify this. You're still carrying a lot of baggage, a lot of bad feelings toward them. You need to deal with this." Even at that early date, Pastor Brafford knew things were changing within our church.

Soon a meeting was arranged. Greg Albrecht and I met with Bill Burns and his pastor for lunch, and Bill was able to talk about some of his pain and hurts. After we were finished, Pastor Brafford asked us a few questions about what we now teach. From then on, he has been a close friend. We often go out to eat, call each other, and pray for each other. It was he who introduced us to John Holland, president of the International Church of the Foursquare Gospel.

From the very beginning, Dr. Holland has been a gracious brother to us. A few years after he got to know us and to understand the changes taking place within our church, he invited us to his denomination's 1996 convention at the Pasadena Civic Center. In one plenary session he told a bit of our story, thanked us for standing up against the state of California when it wanted to begin regulating churches, warmly welcomed us as brothers, and asked me to briefly address the large audience. I was both awed and thrilled as five thousand Foursquare representatives energetically applauded and cheered my brief remarks. I even got a very public hug!

RUTH TUCKER'S EARLY INTEREST

Ruth Tucker is a church historian and visiting professor at Trinity Evangelical Divinity School in Deerfield, Illinois. She is the author of a dozen books, including *Another Gospel: Alternative Religions and the New Age Movement.*

Our contact with Dr. Tucker began when our church relations director, David Hulme, asked his assistant, Michael Snyder, to contact her to update her regarding changes we had made since the publication of her book about cults. Ruth was a gracious and delightful Christian friend from the first phone call. She worked closely with Michael Snyder and David Hulme to bring her book up to date. She became an advocate for the work of the Holy Spirit in our fellowship. She invited David Hulme to be included in a special lecture series at Trinity Evangelical Divinity School.

David presented the Worldwide Church of God, answered questions, explained changes, and cleared up some of the myths about us. No, we didn't sacrifice animals, and no, Garner Ted hadn't been part of our organization since 1978. His presentation was well received. Some evangelicals in attendance told David that they would stop writing negative articles about us.

Dr. Tucker was excited about our reforms and encouraged us in every way she could. We consider her a gift from God.

DAVID NEFF AND *CHRISTIANITY TODAY*

In October 1995, David Neff of *Christianity Today* wrote a short editorial about the reforms that were sweeping our church. He welcomed the new developments and explained:

> CT met with a representative leadership group [from the WCG] several years ago and was convinced of their commitment, both to Christ and to authentic biblical truth.... CT readers will be glad to know that they are no longer considered among the harlot daughters of the Great Whore.
>
> But how will we respond? Sadly, Christians outside the WCG have been suspicious and slow to extend the right hand of fellowship...by and large, Christians have made the WCG journey of faith and doctrine more difficult. CT commends the WCG leadership for its courage in pursuit of truth. Can we now welcome their people into this trans-denominational fellowship we call evangelicalism?[1]

His comments were an enormous encouragement to us and paved the way for a major article by Ruth Tucker in the July 1996 edition of *Christianity Today* on the vast changes in the Worldwide Church of God. Her article was the first full-length treatment of our reform to appear in a major evangelical publication. She began:

> For most of a half-century, no book on cults was complete without a chapter on the Worldwide Church of God (WCG) and its founder, Her-

bert W. Armstrong. The late Walter Martin, in his classic *The Kingdom of the Cults,* devoted 34 pages to the group, documenting how Armstrong borrowed freely from Seventh-day Adventist, Jehovah's Witnesses, and Mormon doctrines. And it was during my own research and writing on cults and new religions in 1988 that I became aware that something unusual was happening.

I had earlier written to the Pasadena headquarters requesting literature and statistics from the WCG but had received no response. Then came that phone call I will never forget. It was from Michael Snyder, assistant to the director of public relations, who had just discovered my letter and was calling to find out if there was still time to incorporate new information into my book.

The conversation that followed was nothing short of astonishing. I knew that Armstrong had died in 1986 and that Joseph Tkach, Sr., had succeeded him as pastor general. But I was not aware of changes that signaled a dramatic turnaround in the church.

From Snyder I learned that books written by Armstrong, once the defining literature of the movement, were being revised or taken out of print. I also learned that Joseph Tkach, Sr., had informed the church membership that he would not shrink from his responsibility to correct any doctrine proven to be in error. But most astonishing was Snyder's own testimony of faith, which convinced me he was a brother in Christ.

In the years following, I have had many more meetings with leaders in the church and have closely followed every change in doctrine and practice that has transformed this heretical sect into an evangelical denomination. I am taken aback by the transparency and open profession of faith by these Christians who, by their own testimony, have come out of a "fog of legalism."[2]

A little later in her article Ruth wrote, "The 'changes'—as they are referred to by insiders—are truly historic. Never before in the history of Christianity has there been such a complete move to orthodox Christianity by an unorthodox fringe church."[3] In a similar vein in another publication she said: "Let this go down forever in history, that a movement outside orthodoxy can turn to God, turn to truth, and hold its name high. As a church historian, I cannot cite anything else like this."[4]

The rest of Ruth's article in *Christianity Today* details many of our doctrinal changes and gives readers a brief historic background of our church. One sidebar to the article especially moved me. Camilla F. Kleindienst, a lifetime member of the WCG, wrote of her struggles with the changes and how she finally came to believe they were of God. She wrote: "I have never seen our congregation this happy and energized. I am living in the most exciting time of my spiritual life because, in a historical event, God laid his hands on our organization and steered us in a direction we had not anticipated to a place us where he wanted us."[5]

I'm grateful for Camilla's honest and encouraging comments. I'm also grateful that God has continued to steer us to new friends who have made our transition easier. One of these new friends is Hank Hanegraaff, president of the Christian Research Institute in Rancho Santa Margarita, California.

HANK HANEGRAAFF'S HELPFUL RESPONSE

As the transformation of our church began to accelerate and increasingly focus on major tenets of faith, David Hulme found himself in a difficult situation. As our director of church relations, he was given the task of articulating what the church believed to the outside world—yet he himself did not believe what the church now taught. (David currently heads the United Church of God, our largest splinter group.) For a year or so, that task fell to Greg Albrecht and Mike Feazell and me. We would contact people who reported about the WCG and say to them, "Look, in your literature you say that we believe X, Y, and Z. Well, we want to update you on what we do believe; we don't believe that anymore. You're publishing information that's ten or twenty years old. Could we update it for you?"

As one thing led to another, we finally said, "You know, Hank Hanegraaff is a person we should talk to. We think he'd listen." We knew about Hank through his radio broadcast, *The Bible Answer Man*. Several of us had been listening to Hank on the radio, as well as to a number of other teachers. Unfortunately, our church at the time was in such turmoil that it was difficult to receive all the nurturing we needed. We were reading people like Chuck Swindoll and Max Lucado and listening to selected radio programs, including Hank's. Greg and Mike were also aware of Hank's ministry, so together we decided to write to him. Here's Greg's letter, dated January 5, 1994:

Dear Mr. Hanegraaff,

May I congratulate you and your staff for the ongoing work of the Christian Research Institute. In addition, I thank you for your work in writing *Christianity in Crisis*. Your book is a valuable contribution and a well-documented resource for the body of Christ.

I am writing to request a favor. As editor of *The Plain Truth* (published by the Worldwide Church of God) I hear from readers who have asked the Christian Research Institute to advise them about our mission and teachings. Last month a reader commented that he no longer wanted to receive *The Plain Truth* because the Christian Research Institute told him that we do not teach the deity of Jesus Christ.

This letter is like others we receive in that it accurately echoes and reflects a past, historical position of the Worldwide Church of God and *The Plain Truth*. I have no quarrel with the fact that the Church's past teaching about the deity of Jesus Christ was woefully inadequate. However, such a statement is most definitely not an accurate representation of our current teaching.

Since Herbert W. Armstrong's death, the Worldwide Church of God has been in the process of examining many fundamental teachings, some of which distanced us from more orthodox Christians. I enclose our most recent edition of *Statement of Beliefs of the Worldwide Church of God*. In addition to our desire for doctrinal and biblical accuracy, the

Worldwide Church of God is redressing the errors of being exclusivist and inbred in our approach to other Christians.

We do not wish to be antagonists with you or the Christian Research Institute. It is our desire to be understood, and to be properly represented. We know that we have made mistakes, and like all Christians, we would like to change some of the things we have said and done in the past. We wish to be viewed and examined on the basis of what we are now preaching and teaching, rather than on the basis of our past.

We realize it is difficult to maintain current files about the teachings of the Worldwide Church of God. Therefore, in order to be of assistance, we would be happy to meet with you or your representatives. We would like to provide current doctrinal information and written statements to help you in your work.

We look forward to meeting with you at your convenience.

Greg R. Albrecht

Editor, *The Plain Truth*

A few days later Hank's office called Greg to set up a meeting. From the first time we met, Hank recognized the enormity of our task and understood that we were facing some tremendous battles. After thoroughly quizzing us about our faith and expressing satisfaction with our answers, he invited us to be guests on his radio program. Our fellowship was not ready for that at the time. Hank understood and said, "Anytime you're ready, you just say the word." We finally appeared on his program a number of months after our initial meeting, and when we did, he introduced us to his listening audience as "brothers in the Lord." We taped for three hours, enough to put together three one-hour programs.

Hank helped us tremendously by letting his many listeners know that something good was happening in the Worldwide Church of God. He was the first one to announce the news to the larger public. He did so not only on his broadcast, but also in print. In a winter 1996 article appearing in the *Christian Research*

Journal, he made the following remarks:

> This is unprecedented in church history. It's the very kind of thing that
> those who have given their lives in ministry to the kingdom of the cults
> hope for. Rather than developing hurdles for these guys to jump over,
> our job is to facilitate the process, recognizing they had an enormous
> tactical problem in winning over their own members. They don't want
> to galvanize people around Garner Ted Armstrong or other splinter
> groups.
>
> Many other Sabbatarian groups have looked to what the Worldwide
> Church of God has done and said, "How did you do this? How do *we*
> do this?" They're charting brand-new territory.[6]

Hank has been a good friend from the beginning of our relationship. He
agreed to be the commencement speaker at the 1996 graduation exercises for
Ambassador College and attended graveside services for my dad. I appreciate the
way he announced my dad's death to his constituents:

> Christians across the globe mourned when Joseph W. Tkach, Sr., leader
> of the Worldwide Church of God (WCG), died on Sept. 23, 1995 of
> complications from cancer. He was 68.
>
> As successor to WCG founder Herbert W. Armstrong, Tkach boldly
> led the Pasadena, California-based church from cultism into Christianity....
>
> [Hank Hanegraaff] praised the late Joseph Tkach, Sr., as "a man who
> risked losing his reputation, his livelihood, his career, and world respect
> in his all-out devotion to finding and proclaiming the truth."[7]

Hank has been a breath of fresh air to us. Not all countercult ministries initially responded to us as he did. He always has been gracious, welcoming, and
encouraging to us, and we thank God for him and his ministry. He is our brother
in the Lord.

GEORGE MATHER EXTENDS HIS HAND

A Lutheran minister and author named George Mather once worked with Walter Martin, Hank's predecessor at the Christian Research Institute. George helped Walter put together his classic work, *TheKingdom of the Cults,* and is the coeditor with Larry A. Nichols of a more recent book called *Dictionary of Cults, Sects, Religions and the Occult.* He and Larry are writing his own book for InterVarsity Press on the changes we've made in the WCG.

George was introduced to us about the same time we were getting to know our Foursquare Gospel friends. George was so moved by what he saw happening among us that he started telling his Lutheran colleagues. Soon we received a call from Al Barry, president of the Missouri Synod Lutheran Church. He wanted to meet us. We flew to St. Louis, where we met with Dr. Barry and other church leaders. We also appeared as guests on Don Matzat's radio program, *Issues, Etc.,* broadcast on the Jubilee Radio Network based in St. Louis.

MORE FRIENDS AT AZUSA PACIFIC

Another organization that should be noted for its help to us is Azusa Pacific University. Our connection with Azusa began when Greg Albrecht started taking classes there back in the late seventies. But perhaps he should tell this part of the story:

> I started going to graduate school at Azusa Pacific (then Azusa Pacific College, now Azusa Pacific University, APU) in 1976. I went at the time because Ambassador College here in Pasadena was pursuing accreditation. I was teaching in the religion department, yet held solely a bachelor of arts from Ambassador itself. I needed at least a master's degree and was asked to get one. I had no idea where to go; I only knew of a few schools I did not want to attend.
>
> When I learned of Azusa Pacific, I found a school that had a high view of the Bible. That was important to me, since I was a traditional

Worldwide Church of God believer. The infallibility and authority of the Bible had always been important to us. But because I was a true believer of Armstrongism, when I went to Azusa I carefully guarded against the "Protestant Theology" I needed to learn for the master's degree I was granted in 1977. I was on guard against what we called at the time "the leaven of intellectualism." I needed the respectability of a degree, but I certainly didn't want any of the beliefs of the historic Christian church, as I see them now.

Mike Feazell began to go to Azusa Pacific in the spring of 1990. Mike, along with his assistant, C. W. Davis, were probably the first people from our fellowship to have a bona-fide educational experience at Azusa (this was a good twelve years after I had gone there). With the death of Mr. Armstrong, Mike and C. W. were free to think thoughts, to embrace questions that I had not been free to think or embrace. They developed relationships with a number of the school's faculty members, people such as Dr. John Hartley, a distinguished Old Testament scholar; Dr. Earl Grant, professor of evangelism and missions; Dr. Lane Scott; Dr. Donald Thorsen; Dr. Les Blank; as well as others at Azusa Pacific. These people embraced Mike and C. W. and identified with what they began to see happening in our church. At that very time, unconnected from their experience, some of us in Pasadena were beginning to go through a dramatic, revolutionary upheaval in our world-view. We were coming to Christ and dealing with issues that were directly challenging our established belief system—biblical views that turned our world upside down (to borrow the phrase from the Book of Acts).

These faculty members and administrators at APU embraced Mike and C. W., as well as other WCG members who began attending, without trying to indoctrinate them. In fact, APU is well known for its tolerance for differing views, while carefully upholding the historic Christian faith. People from several theological streams—Wesleyan,

Friends, Nazarenes—come through the university. The faculty is consistently tolerant without pushing or demanding adherance to certain views.

Staff and faculty at Azusa Pacific understood our situation and were prepared for it, based on their experience with students from various denominations. Of course, we were probably a bigger challenge than most others! Nonetheless, they accepted our people, and this helped us tremendously. For the first time, we were able to debate and work through the issues facing us. Mike Feazell was quite open about what was happening in our fellowship, and the APU faculty rallied to our support, even as they were extremely careful about how they dealt with us. They realized that people both from inside and outside might criticize if they were not careful. Despite their cautious restraint, criticism came.

Some members who left us said: "Those people at Azusa are your consultants. They're rewriting your church doctrines and constitution. You've forgotten Herbert Armstrong and all the truths revealed to him." Almost all our splinter groups see Azusa Pacific as the great Satan. They think of the Azusa people as the evil men who led us away from the teachings of Herbert Armstrong and into the Protestant church. Obviously, such a charge is far from the truth. The staff and faculty at Azusa emphatically *did not* do any such thing. At no time did we ever formally consult with them on doctrinal issues. They refused to meddle with what we were doing, nor did we ask them to do so.

But they did offer friendship. They did come alongside us. They did offer prayers—and for that we will always be thankful. For that Azusa Pacific is to be heartily commended.

SUPPORT AT FULLER SEMINARY

The administrators and faculty at Fuller Seminary also have been helpful to us. Richard Mouw, president of Fuller, said: "I have met with the leadership of the church and without reservation consider them brothers in Christ. I am profoundly moved by their testimonies of what God has done for them personally and in the movement. These people have led the most courageous, inspiring, and Christ-centered movement into biblical Christianity that I have ever seen."[8]

FINDING NEW FRIENDS

After we started making our changes in 1987, God began to introduce us to a number of evangelicals who have become dear friends. Two Foursquare Gospel leaders, Bill Brafford and John Holland, led the way in welcoming us and introducing us to others. Dr. Holland has introduced us to scores of respected evangelical leaders, including such outstanding men as Don Argue at the National Association of Evangelicals and Paul Cedar of Mission America. It was John Holland who opened many of the doors for us into the evangelical world. Without his help, for example, we wouldn't have been introduced to Don Argue. And without Don's help, we might still be struggling with a difficult publications problem.

When *The Plain Truth* went from being a freely distributed denominational magazine that promoted the WCG as the "one and only true church" to a paid subscription Christian magazine, we had to advertise to make ends meet. But when we tried to take out advertising in the normal evangelical outlets, we were greeted with a lot of closed doors. By then *Christianity Today* had published a major article by Ruth Tucker outlining and applauding the changes within the WCG.

Word didn't seem to be reaching most of the evangelical public. We had a terrible time trying to convince potential advertisers, as well as magazines in which we wanted to advertise, that we were for real. "Well, maybe you're for real," we'd hear, "but we're sorry. You can't advertise here. We still have a lot of subscribers who have deep feelings against your group, and we can't risk it."

In the fall of 1996, *Charisma* magazine was considering whether to take advertisements promoting Plain Truth Ministries. When a staff member called Don Argue to inquire about us, he told them, "I can vouch for them. Take the ad. They're for real." We're deeply grateful to God for all these friends and for the new friends we continue to meet. We were especially gratified in November

1996 that the Evangelical Christian Publishing Association welcomed our Plain Truth Ministries into membership. At that time I felt constrained to quote from the March 1996 edition of *The Plain Truth* magazine:

> We've been wrong. There was never an intent to mislead anyone. We were so focused on what we believed we were doing for God that we didn't recognize the spiritual path we were on. Intended or not, that path was not the biblical one.
>
> So we stand today at the foot of the cross—the ultimate symbol of all reconciliation. It is the common ground on which estranged and alienated parties can meet. As Christians, we all identify with the suffering that took place there, and we hope that identification will bring us together.

I'm not certain the ECPA was right when it said in its November 11, 1996, newsletter, *Footprints,* that "the journey of the Worldwide Church of God is indeed the top religious story of this decade," but I am full of gratitude that we can now address one another as brothers. Yet there is work to do, especially in convincing people that the best response to news of our changes is *not,* "Yeah, right."

DOCTRINE: SOMETIMES EASIER TO TEACH THAN TO DO

Greg Albrecht and I attended the Mission America meeting in Washington, D.C., in May 1996. The guest speaker for the day was the energetic president of Moody Bible Institute, Dr. Joseph Stowell. Joe Stowell delivered a powerful message about how Christians need to recognize the barriers that stand between their different traditions in order to get beyond those barriers and enjoy rich Christian fellowship. He spoke of one friend in a tradition different from his own whom he was getting to know better. In a phone conversation, Joe Stowell asked the man what his children were going to do for Halloween. What costumes would they wear? After a short silence, the man replied, "Joe, we don't do that in our denomination. We don't celebrate Halloween because of its pagan roots."

Dr. Stowell was not at all offended but asked, "Well, what will you be doing with the kids?"

"Oh, we'll be going out to eat and then take our kids to a movie," the man replied.

With a loud chuckle Joe Stowell responded, "Well, we don't do *that*. Our tradition doesn't believe in going to movies.

His point, of course, was that we shouldn't let our traditions and backgrounds get in the way of genuine Christian fellowship based solely on our trust in the atoning death of Christ. We are all one at the foot of the cross. It was a tremendous message that greatly encouraged us.

Afterward I had the opportunity to meet Dr. Stowell. As I shook his hand, I introduced myself by saying, "I'm with the Worldwide Church of God." In that instant his face fell and his expression visibly changed, almost as if to say, "Should I really be here, shaking this guy's hand? I mean, this guy is with the Worldwide Church of God!" When I proceeded to compliment him on his great message, it wasn't hard to tell that a good deal of dissonance was exploding in his brain.

I could see the turmoil in his mind. The irony of giving *that* message and then, immediately afterward, having to shake the hand of the president and pastor general of the Worldwide Church of God! Although I wanted to say something, the decorum of the moment prevented me from doing so. What preacher hasn't given a message that he found more difficult to apply than to deliver? Besides, perhaps he hadn't heard the news about us. Or perhaps he had received conflicting reports and concluded the news was "too good to be true." I'm sure that Joe Stowell and I will have occasion to talk again and recount this brief discussion!

I don't blame anyone for being cautious about accepting the idea that the Worldwide Church of God is now thoroughly evangelical. Joseph Stowell is not the only one who has been shocked to meet members and pastors of the Worldwide Church of God in places like Promise Keepers, interfaith prayer breakfasts, and Christian relief efforts. We are beginning to learn that genuine

Christian fellowship is not based on goodwill or great hopes, but on agreement concerning the person and work of Jesus Christ.

THE CENTRAL ROLE OF PRAYER

It was such a refreshing experience for us to meet people like Kevin Mannoia, the superintendent of the Free Methodist Church in Southern California, who gave us unconditional fellowship and prayerful support during certain administrative crises that faced us. Or like the Southern Baptist who recently said to me, "Brother, I hear what's happening with you. Can I pray with you?"

You bet you can! Especially because our recent journey has shown us what astonishing power there is in believing prayer! How have these radical changes in the Worldwide Church of God come about? What prompted them? What motivated them? When all the analyses have been done and the sociological studies have been completed and the surveys taken and tabulated, I'm convinced one factor stands miles above them all: prayer. What has happened in the WCG is a sovereign move of God, prompted in large measure by the believing prayers of people concerned about the welfare of one little part of God's church.

We continue to hear stories of men and women who have prayed for years, even decades, that God would do a miracle and reform our church. Despite the long years of apparent divine silence and regardless of the hostility they may have felt from our members, they continued to pray. Finally, God answered.

A letter to the editor from David Scott in the March 1997 issue of *Charisma* says, "We were once members of the Worldwide Church of God with Herbert W. Armstrong. It is wonderful to hear that they have seen the light. It has been my prayer that God would turn them from the teaching of a man to the teaching of Jesus! We wept when we heard that they have repented. Let's keep praying and see what God will do."[9]

Don Mears, a long time WCG pastor, said: "During the late 1970s I was preparing for a Bible study series on the Epistle to the Romans and began to study the epistle in more depth than I ever had before. I was dismayed at what I found, as I began to realize how far our preaching and practice in the church had strayed into legalism and away from the gospel of grace that Paul described. Ever since that time, my wife and I have been praying for the church to come to a deeper understanding of the grace of God."[10]

Jack Hayford, a prominent evangelical and pastor, addressed leading ministers and regional pastors of the WCG in Pasadena on March 18, 1997. In his closing remarks he said that one day more than a dozen years ago one of the former elders in his church, John Darnell, called him and asked if he would accompany him to a particular spot to pray. "Where?" Dr. Hayford asked. "I don't even know why I feel this prompting from the Lord," John replied, "but do you know where the Worldwide Church of God offices are? I feel as if I'm supposed to go over there and walk around that place and just pray." So that's what they did. Dr. Hayford and John Darnell drove over to our offices, parked nearby, and prayed as they walked inconspicuously around the campus. Their visit came very early on a Saturday morning so almost no one was around. When they finished, they got back in their car and left.

As he was wrapping up his comments to us, Dr. Hayford said, "You can't help but wonder—how many people did God move to pray for you? We actually walked around this place. I sensed then that if someone is willing to do a little thing, then God is willing to do a big thing. It's like Israel when the people walked around Jericho and God won the battle. The walls fell down, didn't they?"

Yes, they did. Thank God they did! In the past few years we have heard many reports from people who tell us they've been praying for a move of the Spirit in our midst for a long time. O, how glad we are that God answers prayer!

CHAPTER FIVE

CONSPIRACY
THEORIES AND
REJECTION

J ust before he died in January 1986, Herbert Armstrong told his handpicked successor—my father, Joseph Tkach Sr.—that changes needed to be made in the church. Mr. Armstrong never detailed everything that he meant, but it was clear even then that the church's stance on medicine and use of doctors was at the forefront of his mind. At that point in our history, it was commonly believed that people of real faith had no need of doctors and medicine. Yet in the years preceding his death, Mr. Armstrong himself frequently took advantage of modern medicine. This conflict led us to want to revisit the church's official position on the issue.

Within a year of Mr. Armstrong's death, church leadership began an intensive study of the WCG's practice and doctrine. No one had any particular agenda in mind, nor did anyone have any specific goals in view other than to identify, if possible, what changes Mr. Armstrong might have had in mind before his death.

Beginning in 1987, a series of changes slowly began to be made in the church—unsystematic, unplanned, often in response to persistent questions by the membership. My dad worked very closely with his top advisers in studying questions that were raised and in correcting erroneous teaching. Therefore a sizable faction of the church—members and ministers who did not approve of the changes—chose to believe that his advisers (a "gang of four," a "band of three," "three stooges") were making these changes without my father's knowledge or approval.

When my dad did give a major sermon on doctrinal changes, he always read major portions of it, confirming in these people's minds that he was a mere dupe of the "gang of four." They circulated rumors that others were writing his articles for church publications and publishing them either without his knowledge or against his will. These folks would say things like, "Some wicked men behind the scenes are forging Mr. Tkach's signature. He doesn't really go along with all this stuff. He doesn't really believe all this new teaching. We don't know why he's doing it. Maybe they're blackmailing him. Who knows what's happening? This can't be real. Herbert Armstrong's successor could not be saying all these things. Something's up. We need to get rid of people like Joe Jr., Mike Feazell, Greg Albrecht, Bernie Schnippert, Kyriacos Stavrinides, and people like that. Then the truth will prevail." In fact some who eventually left the WCG made us an offer. The tentative amount to buy out several of us was two million dollars.

Of course, the reason my dad read his sermons had nothing to do with conspiracies. Like many of us, when speaking extemporaneously he would sometimes make errors and inadvertently use some of the nomenclature and phraseology of the past in trying to explain what we had now come to believe. Every denomination has its own jargon, and these terms just trip off the tongue. Whenever my dad would make a mistake in speaking publicly, people would exclaim, "Aha! He *doesn't* know what he's talking about!" So shortly after he took over leadership of the church, he started to read almost every word he spoke in public.

It didn't seem to occur to people that if my dad didn't like or agree with material Mike Feazell (who was his executive assistant and editorial adviser) or others prepared for him, he could have changed it or not used it at all. Those who knew my dad know that he definitely had a mind of his own. My dad hired

Mike Feazell to assist him, especially in writing and theology, and he could have fired him at any time. My dad spent hours every day with Mike, working out details of letters, articles, and sermons. Every article went through an approval cycle that included a review process which requested comments and suggested edits from virtually all top ministers and advisers in Pasadena, even those who opposed the changes. My dad reviewed all the comments before approving his material for publication. Nothing was published in my dad's name that he had not personally studied, discussed, and approved.

Nevertheless, many of our members didn't believe that the changes they were seeing in the church were real. Just as evangelicals have a hard time believing that the Worldwide Church of God has moved into orthodoxy, many of our members had a hard time believing their church was moving away from its peculiar doctrinal distinctives.

THREE CONSPIRACY THEORIES

When the church began making doctrinal reforms, some of the people closest to my dad couldn't accept that he was behind them; the only way they could cope was to develop conspiracy theories that "explained" what was *really* going on. There were three main ones:

1. One former senior minister advanced the theory that Greg Albrecht, Mike Feazell, and I were acting out our revenge against the church for the abusive way we were treated as we grew up. We are all graduates of our church's high school (Imperial) and college (Ambassador).

All I can say about this is that proclaiming the gospel of grace certainly is an unusual way to get revenge. Would to God all "revenge" was so sweet!

2. David Hulme, formerly our director of church relations, developed another theory. He grew close to my dad and for a time was one of our presenters on *The World Tomorrow* television program. When God began to change my

dad, David theorized that my dad had all these doctrinal reforms in his mind for ten or fifteen years and was just patiently waiting for the moment when he could mobilize his plan of reform.

In his resignation letter dated April 17, 1995, David outlined a number of what he called "contradictions and inconsistencies" and concluded by saying:

> I have tried very hard to support you for nine years despite the almost constant reversals and contradictions. It is with profound sorrow and regret that I have to tell you that I can no longer walk alongside you because we are not agreed on what I believe to be some of the fundamentals of Christian belief and practice. I look forward to the day when we can walk together.
>
> Effective Wednesday, April 19, 1995, I am resigning from my employment with the Worldwide Church of God and its affiliates, as well as from the boards of the same....
>
> So that there will be no misunderstanding I am sending this document to twelve people known to me for their integrity and honesty. They will serve as witnesses to the content and intent of this memo.

My father responded in a letter nine days later:

> Dear Dave,
> It is with regret that I accept your resignation, and with sorrow that I read your false accusations and misrepresentations. It is further disappointing that you chose to share your letter of resignation with a dozen people who are, as you put it, known to you "for their integrity and honesty," but at least one of whom (if it was not you) allowed your misleading, if not distorted, perspective to be distributed around the world.
>
> You accused me of having had a hidden "agenda of doctrinal changes." Dave, there has been no "agenda" set by humans. But that does not mean that as Christ opens our eyes we can't see more. The

more the Holy Spirit led us into truth, the more we could see needed to be changed. The Holy Spirit set the agenda, not me. In April of 1994, I had no idea that the Holy Spirit would lead me to see that we had been wrong in our understanding of the old and new covenants and the implications of that fact on our understanding of Sabbath and Holy Day observance, clean and unclean meat and triple tithing. In hindsight, I can see now that there was indeed an agenda, but it was Christ's agenda.

You seem to feel you have discovered some astounding revelation when you point out that last year I explained the Christian's relationship to the law one way, and then at a certain point this year began explaining it another way. I don't deny that. I began explaining it correctly as soon as Christ opened my mind to understand it correctly. That is what I firmly believe Christ would expect me or anyone else to do, and I firmly believe it was Christ who led me, for the sake of the Church, down the road to understanding him as he is revealed in Scripture.

You have twisted and misrepresented my comment that the recent changes have "been in my mind" since the 1970s to mean that I understood, believed and embraced these things at that time and have kept that fact a secret ever since. That is not what I was conveying to you, and it surprises me that you took it that way. I was trying to point out to you that challenges about the validity of certain doctrines, challenges that were raised by leading ministers of the Church in the 1970s, caused me to realize that there were indeed doctrinal questions that had never been adequately answered. Chief among these questions was that of a clear biblical basis for determining which Old Testament laws were binding on Christians and which were not. (Surely you are aware that we have in the past, as only one example, believed it was a sin for a Christian to wear clothes made of mixed fabrics.) My response at the time, however, was to simply put the subject "on the shelf" and give it little thought until years later, when I found myself, as Pastor General, responsible for the spiritual instruction of the Church and challenged on many of the same points. I did not embrace those ideas at the time, and I continued wholeheartedly and conscientiously to support Mr. Armstrong and to preach and teach the Church's position in every way, believing there were indeed answers to any and every potential objection. Even though I realized there were questions that had never been adequately answered, and this nagging realization troubled me, I still believed the Church was correct and that answers must exist. For you to construe this as some underhanded plot is simply preposterous....

You are right that Mr. Armstrong wanted his successor to continue the Church's preparation for Christ's return. And that is precisely what Christ has been gracious enough to allow me to have a part in doing. By God's grace, the Church is closer to Jesus Christ than it has ever been. The Church is the Body of Christ. It exists to bring glory to him, not to me or to Mr. Armstrong. I uphold Jesus Christ, first and foremost, and may it always be so.

Dave, maybe you are right about our not being agreed in the first place. Apparently, you were looking for someone to uphold Mr. Armstrong. But Mr. Armstrong's concern was to appoint someone who would, in the final analysis, uphold Christ. By the grace and mercy of God, our Savior has seen fit to count me worthy of the privilege of upholding the name of Jesus Christ and his gospel at all costs.

> In Christ's love and service,
> Joseph W. Tkach

David's letter of resignation came in stark contrast to another memo he had written almost nine years before. On May 27, 1986, David wrote to my dad, the newly installed pastor general:

On or about Sunday, September 15, 1985, Mr. Herbert Armstrong and I had a discussion regarding my wife's then-precarious health. I spent about one hour with him, the second half of which he devoted to a discussion of his successor. He told me that he would be discussing this with a number of leading men in Pasadena. I had the impression that I was the first in a series of discussions he would have.

He then listed a number of men and rather plainly told me of his objections to all and asked me what I thought. He then said he had concluded that you, Joseph Tkach, would be his successor and asked me how did I think that would work. I told him that I thought that he had made the best choice and that I would fully support you.

Today David is the leader of the United Church of God, the largest of the splinter groups (with about seventeen thousand members).

3. A third conspiracy theory supposed that Mike Feazell or I had obtained some kind of scandalous information about my father that we were holding over his head to manipulate him. They thought that we—or alternately that Greg Albrecht, Bernie Schnippert, Kyriacos Stavrinides, or any of several others— would use this information to get our way whenever my dad was especially opposed to some proposed change. Like the other wild theories, this one had zero basis in fact.

Perhaps one of the more interesting facts about all three of these conspiracy theories is that the men who developed them are now leading the main splinter groups. It's mighty tempting to build my own theory about that fact, but in view of my own experience with conspiracy theories, I think it might be best to leave it alone.

MEMBERSHIP AND FINANCIAL LOSSES

The Worldwide Church of God reached its peak attendance in 1988—two years after Mr. Armstrong's death—with 126,800 members and 150,000 in attendance. Those figures stayed relatively stable until 1992, when a slight dip was noted. By 1994 church attendance had slipped to 109,600…and then came the Christmas Eve sermon. In the year following that milestone message, attendance plummeted to 66,400 members, and by the time of this writing it had leveled off at around 58,000.

Our membership losses have resulted in a corresponding drop in income. Receipts worldwide in 1990 amounted to more than $211 million. By 1994, the year immediately preceding "The Sermon," income stood at about $164.6 million. The following year income dropped to $103.4 million. In this past year our receipts totaled about $68.5 million. We expect a national income of $38 million in 1997.

With dramatically fewer members and greatly reduced income, expenses had to be cut as well. In 1986, our total expenses came to more than $131 million. By 1996 our total budgeted expenses fell to about $52.5 million. We were forced to lay off most of our headquarters staff, cut circulation of *The Plain Truth* magazine, sharply reduce subsidies to Ambassador University, end our acclaimed performing arts series at Ambassador Auditorium, and sell off many of our assets. In addition, we put up for sale our fifty-one-acre Pasadena world headquarters, and financial realities dictated that we do the same with our Ambassador University campus in Big Sandy, Texas.

So you do the math. What do these figures tell you? If the changes in the Worldwide Church of God are some kind of con job—some cynical, conspiratorial plot hatched in secret back rooms—then we're not very adept at pulling it off. We should never have hired a public relations firm to "turn us into a mainstream church" (a patently false rumor circulated, no doubt, by ex-members trying to make sense of our dramatic doctrinal changes). At any time in the past several years we could have called a halt to the changes, turned back the clock, confessed that we were wrong, and tried to woo back disaffected members (along with their pocketbooks). Yet we have not done that and we will not do that.

Why not?

Because we have come to believe with all our hearts that a vital, vibrant, growing relationship with the Lord Jesus Christ is worth any cost we may be required to pay. "What good is it," the Master still asks, "if a man should gain the whole world and lose his own soul?" We have counted the cost, and we are not going back. Our hearts resonate with the apostle Paul, who wrote, "I consider everything a loss compared to the surpassing greatness of knowing Christ Jesus my Lord, for whose sake I have lost all things. I consider them rubbish, that I may gain Christ and be found in him, not having a righteousness of my own that comes from the law, but that which is through faith in Christ—the righteousness that comes from God and is by faith. I want to know Christ and the power of his resurrection and the fellowship of sharing in his sufferings, becoming like him in his death, and so, somehow, to attain to the resurrection from the dead" (Philippians 3:8–11).

NOT ALL COSTS ARE FINANCIAL

In the past few years I've come to understand more clearly than I ever desired what Paul meant when he spoke of "the fellowship of sharing in [Christ's] sufferings." Some of my friends from high school and college days think I'm demon-possessed. If they don't go that far, at least they're convinced I was never really converted. Most of them won't talk to me. And those who do talk to me often tell me things I'm not so sure I want to hear. One longtime friend, a man I've known since high school, recently left us to join one of our splinter groups. Upon his departure he told me, "Boy, it's amazing, Joe, how many people just can't stand you and Mike. They hate you. They're really angry." I wanted to say several things, but I bit my tongue.

Our offices continue to receive a steady stream of angry letters (usually anonymous) which denounce us for leaving "the truth" and embracing Protestant lies. Some are very artistic. I received one recently that included a nasty but extremely creative cartoon. It shows a picture of my dad working marionette strings attached to Mr. Armstrong, while I'm working other strings attached to my dad. The cartoon labels me "Jereboam Jr."

Of course I'm not the only one singled out for such letters. Greg Albrecht, who heads Plain Truth Ministries, not long ago received a long, vitriolic five-page missive that blasted him for every sin in the book. The writer went on and on, wringing him out in vituperative language. At the bottom of the letter the author signed off, "May you burn in hell, Your brother in Christ." (Who says Christian brotherhood is dead?)

One man who identified himself as a member of one of our splinter groups (the Global Church of God) visited our worship service in Pasadena in the spring of 1997. After services he approached me, tapped me on the shoulder, and announced his name and church affiliation. He then told me that if he "had the authority" he would kill me. In front of many others he declared that he would like to cut my head off.

Long before I really started feeling the heat, my dad found himself thrown in the furnace. He passed away in September 1995 from cancer, but I'm convinced his health declined much faster than it would have ordinarily. The enormous amount of stress he faced from leading the church into reform helped send him to an early grave (but into the Master's arms!)

The personal costs don't stop there. Members of my own extended family left our church to join one of the splinter groups which has been somewhat hostile toward us. One of my relatives simply cannot understand what has happened within the WCG. She has been angry, hurt, and confused about the changes. She saw them as a betrayal. We have tried to talk about these issues a number of times, but we simply no longer see eye to eye. "But Joe," she will plead, "don't you see that the Sabbath is the right way to love God?"

"I understand that it is one acceptable means to love God," I say, "but if you approach it as a necessary means—as a way to earn His acceptance and use it as the measure of authentic Christianity—then you've gotten off track."

These are but a few of the examples in my own experience of what it means to "share in the fellowship of his sufferings." It has not been easy. It has not been pleasant. It has not led to long nights of restful sleep or carefree days of blissful ease.

But it has been worth it! I agree wholeheartedly with another of Paul's memorable sentences: "I consider that our present sufferings are not worth comparing with the glory that will be revealed in us" (Romans 8:18). No, they're not worth the comparison at all! And in any event, suffering is only part of the story. There also has been real joy.

REACTION FROM FORMER MEMBERS

The reaction to all this from those who have left us is both interesting and sad. I have been told many times, "You guys make us sick. You're just going to the world and to these harlot daughters to seek approval." We have tried to explain that we're really not running around seeking the approval of men, that the only One we actively seek to please is God. "But you know the way it works in a family," I'll say. "When someone in a family does something that's good for the family, all the other family members rejoice and want to come alongside. That's what has been happening."

Sadly, many of our former members don't see that…yet. We're praying that God will continue to open eyes, that His light will shine in the hearts of many of those who have left us. We will continue to pray, believing that if our heavenly Father can work one miracle among us, He can do another. Or as many as it takes.

Because that's the kind of God we now know Him to be.

CHAPTER SIX

A SERVANT
OF THE PEOPLE

It had been a long, grueling, and even frightening battle. But on October 15, 1980, the state of California dropped its much-publicized lawsuit against the Worldwide Church of God—a suit that had jeopardized every American's Constitutional First Amendment rights to free expression of religion. Stanley R. Rader, at that time the WCG's treasurer and general counsel, had led the legal fight against the state's attempt to seize control of our church. He had won. Yet because some observers insinuated that he led the battle only for personal gain— that he might become the leading candidate to replace Herbert Armstrong as head of the WCG—on January 8, 1981, Rader published a large advertisement in the Los Angeles *Times* and in the Pasadena *Star-News* to announce his resignation from official church positions and to make the following statement:

> I do not consider it even remotely possible that I will succeed Mr. Armstrong. I am not worthy. I am not qualified to serve Christ in that way. I do not believe it is my calling. It certainly is not my desire. And I do not believe it is God's will.... I do not expect anyone to succeed Mr. Armstrong. The Living God has entrusted Mr. Armstrong with a Great Commission and God has never taken a man before his work was done. I do not look for or expect another pastor general.[1]

Herbert Armstrong himself not only strongly defended Rader against his detractors, but also agreed that there would be no pastor general to succeed the church's founder:

> And brethren, I have to say to you, no one is going to succeed me.... I think that when God lets me die, the thing He's called me for will have been completed, preparing the way for the Second Coming of Christ carrying that Gospel of the Kingdom to the world for a witness to all nations.... If I have been someone in the power and the spirit of Elijah, remember there is no prophecy that God will have an Elisha following Elijah. There is no one in the Church that has the qualifications, the experience that could carry on the work that God has given me to do.[2]

Yet less than five years later, just months before his death, Mr. Armstrong reversed himself and named Joseph Tkach Sr.—my father—to follow him as the next pastor general of the Worldwide Church of God. It was not a choice that many expected. Why was he chosen?

RALLYING THE WIDOWS

The explanation begins on January 3, 1979. That was the day that officers of the state of California, at the direction of Attorney General George Deukmejian, walked into our church offices, took over the operations of our church, and put it in receivership. Deukmejian had charged the WCG with several financial illegalities and had claimed authority to intervene. This was a landmark battle involving constitutional law. Many churches around the nation filed amicus briefs with the court to defend the constitutional separation of church and state. Finally, in October 1980, California Governor Jerry Brown signed into law Senate Bill No. 1493, stripping the attorney general of all powers he had claimed over the church. Soon afterward all suits were dismissed. In the end, the hard-fought case contributed to the protection of all churches...and the WCG was completely exonerated from any wrongdoing.

In a surprising development, my dad became a key figure in opposing this illegal court action. He effectively rallied the congregations in Southern California and the WCG membership—especially its senior citizens—to take action. My dad rose from relative obscurity to meet the frightening challenge. His ultimate effectiveness brought him to the attention of Mr. Armstrong. Subsequent to the court battle, Mr. Armstrong appointed my dad to be director of ministerial services (or church adminstration) of the WCG. It became his job to oversee the church's ministers worldwide. Also at that time he was ordained as an evangelist, historically viewed as the highest ministerial position in the WCG.

This explains only part of my dad's rise to prominence in the WCG. What did he do? Where did he come from? Just who was this man who would succeed Herbert Armstrong as pastor general of the Worldwide Church of God?

MY FATHER'S ROOTS

My dad was born at his parents' Chicago home on March 16, 1927. As was common in those days, the doctor didn't get around to filling out a birth certificate until a few months after my dad's birth. Joseph was the youngest of five children and the only son of William and Mary Tkach, who had emigrated from Carpatho-Russia.

Along with his siblings, my dad grew up in the Russian Orthodox faith. At an early age he became an altar boy, not because he was serious about it, but because that was the thing to do. He graduated from Tilden High School in southwest Chicago and continued to live in the Windy City until he joined the U.S. Navy. He served on two ships, the USS *Jupiter* and the USS *Austin*, a destroyer escort. He fought in World War II and earned two ribbons, including a Victory ribbon for his service in the Pacific theater. After his honorable discharge he returned home and married my mother. If asked about his faith at that time, he would reply, "I'm a member of the Orthodox Church"; yet he was not an active member.

Despite this religious indifference, the family continued to attend the Russian Orthodox Church while visiting a variety of churches in search of greater truth. A growing dissatisfaction eventually blossomed into action. My grandparents often asked questions of their priest, but he never provided answers that satisfied them. Soon the family (except for my dad) began listening to Herbert W. Armstrong on the radio. My dad was not the least bit interested; on the contrary, this new interest in Herbert W. Armstrong bothered him, although he didn't want to argue with his father about it.

One event changed all that. In those days my dad suffered from severe ulcers and was considering surgery to correct the problem. He was on a special bland diet—milk products, baby food, and absolutely nothing spicy. My mother suggested that God could heal him if he allowed himself to be anointed by a WCG minister. While he was very skeptical about the chances for success, he finally agreed to try. A minister was called to anoint my dad—who was astonished to find himself suddenly and miraculously cured of his ulcers. To test this miracle he hurried out to a restaurant where he ordered the spiciest, hottest bowl of chili he could find. In the past, a meal like that could debilitate him for a full day or two, but this time the chili caused him no problems at all. Never again did ulcers give him a moment's trouble. From that point forward, pizza laden with jalapeños and anchovies was one of his favorite meals.

This remarkable incident convinced my dad to become active in his new faith. Yet for a while, despite his intense interest, he was not allowed to attend services. Back in the fifties prospective members couldn't attend the WCG (then called the Radio Church of God) until they had learned a good deal of church doctrine. He became an eager learner, and by January 1961 he was ordained a deacon. From the beginning he showed a willing heart for service. In June 1963 he was ordained to the ministry and over the succeeding years built a solid reputation as "the widows' elder." If a widow (or widower) needed anything, my dad would generally be quick to help meet the need. He'd gladly round up volunteers to paint a house or fix a kitchen appliance or repair some plumbing. Whatever needed to be done, he was available to help.

In 1966 our family moved to Pasadena so my parents could attend Ambassador College. They took classes for three years, intending upon graduation that my dad be sent out to pastor a church. Instead, he remained in Pasadena and eventually pastored a church there.

He spent more than half his ministry in Pasadena and became known as a servant of the people, especially of the senior citizens. He was always available for prayer, visiting and anointing the sick, and ministries of service. He continued to distinguish himself as a minister with a servant's heart. Later, as pastor general, one of his main themes to the pastors was, "We're shepherds, not sheriffs." He and others recognized that there was far too much authoritarianism in the ministerial ranks, and he took steps to try to curb as much of that as possible. No doubt this became a chief concern of his because such destructive authoritarianism had already touched his own family. Many of the ministers who graduated to the authoritarian leadership style found themselves more comfortable in our splinter groups.

A RAPID ASCENSION

At the time my father was appointed to succeed Mr. Armstrong, Dad was heading up church administration. He already was supervising our ministers, so he was a natural candidate. After six and a half years in that position, he was a known commodity and had held every possible ministerial position in our hierarchy. The others who might also have been candidates were quickly stricken from Mr. Armstrong's list.

In the months prior to his death, Herbert Armstrong had spent time individually with each member of the advisory council of elders, telling them specifically whom he didn't want to be chosen. One time when they had all assembled, he said, "Never is my son, Ted, *ever* to be in a position of authority. Not ever."

Privately, he also told several leaders that Rod Meredith should never be in that position. Before he died, Mr. Armstrong decided that he didn't want to let the council pick his successor. One day he got them all together and said, "I'm naming Joseph Tkach as my successor." Nobody disagreed. He died just weeks after all the paperwork had been drawn up to properly document my dad as his successor.

It all happened so quickly. One pastor from Montgomery, Alabama, called our Pasadena headquarters early one morning to confirm the rumor he had heard about the appointment of Joseph Tkach Sr. as Mr. Armstrong's successor. Just after 8:00 A.M., he got Mr. Armstrong's secretary on the line. "Could you please tell me if the rumor is true?" he asked. The woman began crying and replied, "Yes, it is true. Herbert Armstrong has died!" And that wasn't even why he was calling! The story illustrates the closeness in time between the decision which had been legally formalized and Herbert Armstrong's death.

This also brings up a very interesting question about God's providence. If the decision about a successor had been left to someone else, where would we be today?

A NICE HONEYMOON

My dad enjoyed a "honeymoon" for a few years after Mr. Armstrong died. In his first two years, the membership and attendance statistics continued to grow. People trusted my dad, and as the church began to make changes, they wanted to believe these things were right—but the rubber band kept stretching and stretching until finally it broke.

Initially, many of the changes were administrative, especially in the area of how we spent money. While Mr. Armstrong spent freely, my dad tightened the reins a bit. For example, Mr. Armstrong was well known for traveling all around the globe, visiting dignitaries and heads of state. He would talk to them about a "strong hand from someplace" that would one day solve the problems of their nations, referring obliquely to God. Many members found Mr. Armstrong's indirect approach frustrating.

My dad continued the tradition of traveling, but instead of visiting world leaders, he visited all our congregations worldwide. He managed to visit about 98 percent of them in the first four or five years he served as pastor general. This was a very unifying thing; he stressed the theme that we are a spiritual family. Everywhere he went he promoted that theme of unity. And at least for a while, it bore good fruit.

NOT A THEOLOGIAN

My dad was not known as a theologian. This concerned some members. They worried that the church could make significant theological corrections without my dad endorsing them personally. It was my dad's style to publish an article announcing a change and then delegate to others the teaching of it. In the past, Herbert Armstrong always taught everything. Whether he originated the teaching or not, he didn't allow anyone else to reveal anything new. He always presented himself as the source (even though he wasn't on many things) and as the primary expert.

When my dad came along and allowed others to do most of the teaching on major doctrinal changes, some of our members who were used to doctrinal changes coming directly from the top were disconcerted. They would say, "Does he really understand these changes? After all, he's not teaching them; somebody else is. He's letting somebody else answer our questions."

Often my dad was criticized for not giving a sermon about a particular change of doctrine or practice himself. Eventually he responded to these criticisms by speaking from extensive notes; he wanted to avoid stating doctrine inaccurately. But this also meant he was tied firmly to his notes. Then critics started saying that either he didn't understand the new changes or that he didn't agree with them. Otherwise, why would he be so anchored to his notes?

We were breaking so many paradigms. We were not only correcting some of our doctrine (which the church had a long history of doing), we were doing it in a new way.

MY DAD'S LAST YEARS

Over the last three to four years of my dad's life, he became increasingly aware that some of the foundational beliefs underlying the doctrines formerly taught by the WCG were shaky at best. He came to see that some of our world-view and perspectives on church history were not grounded in reality or truth. The idea that the gospel wasn't preached since A.D. 53, for example, he saw as untenable. He also saw problems with British-Israelism and other esoteric doctrines.

Throughout his nine years as pastor general, his most earnest desire was to follow Christ faithfully. He began to present the truth as it unfolded for him; never was there an agenda. Frankly, neither he nor we were smart enough to create such an agenda. Once he announced the first change, however, it was as if someone had stepped on the gas pedal—someone other than us. A flood of questions started pouring in from our ministers and membership. As we answered those questions, more questions came in. There was no way to stop them. The questions spanned the spectrum of doctrine. We were unable to develop a grand scheme for answering them all; we simply had to respond to the questions, one by one, as they came in. We did a lot of research and replied with the most honest answers we could give.

Early on, there were some astute members who saw that the first two or three changes we made required that other changes would soon have to be made. They accurately predicted most of the corrections we announced in the following three or four years. Yet at the time we saw none of this. These people would make their predictions, and we would reply: "That's silly. Why are you saying we're going to change things that have been integral to our identity as a denomination?" We steadfastly denied we were even thinking about such changes, for the simple reason that we weren't considering any such thing. But as time went on and we answered more questions, we ended up making some of the very changes our critics had predicted. It looked as if they had more credibility than we did; I freely admit it appeared as though we really did have some sort of hidden agenda, that we weren't telling the whole story.

For my dad, this reform was literally a life-and-death struggle. On the one hand, he began seeing that one change after another needed to be made. On the other hand, close friends and associates tried to persuade him that these changes were wrong, that more time was needed to study them. Some of his closest personal friends wanted him to go slowly with change or not to make any decisions at all. He was torn between presenting the truth he was discovering and keeping the loyalty and respect of his friends. His experience was much like experiences our members have had.

I'm happy that he made the right choice. He chose biblical truth rather than mere church tradition, even if some critics loudly disagreed with him and insinuated he didn't know what was really going on.

Such voices were forced to change their theories after the Christmas Eve sermon of 1994. After that, it was impossible to claim that my dad misunderstood what he was saying or that he was merely a puppet mouthing the words of conspirators behind the scenes. It was clear the changes in our church were real and that they were here to stay. Membership and financial contributions plummeted steeply and rapidly after the sermon, but my dad refused to budge from where the Spirit of God had so graciously led him.

I have no doubt that the extreme difficulty of those days hastened his death on September 23, 1995, of complications from cancer. He was sixty-eight years old. Before he died, he named me as his successor—and I will never forget either his courage or his example. I now carry the title of president and pastor general of the Worldwide Church of God, and I vividly remember and try to practice one of my dad's most enduring lessons: I am a shepherd, not a sheriff, and I serve a God of grace, not merely a Lord of laws.

That's a lesson I intend to pass along.

CHAPTER SEVEN

WHAT
WE BELIEVED

A lifelong evangelical who recently has become my friend told me a story that highlights the extensive doctrinal and theological changes we've been making the last several years in the Worldwide Church of God. My friend was sitting in a waiting room a few months ago when he noticed a copy of *The Plain Truth* lying on a table. He was acquainted with the magazine and knew of many of our former doctrinal aberrations. Out of curiosity he picked up the magazine. As he skimmed article after article, he became increasingly alarmed. What made him so anxious?

"I thought I was losing my theological discernment," he explained. "I had heard nothing of the changes taking place within the Worldwide Church of God, and I was startled—no, worried—that I couldn't find anything doctrinally wrong with the articles I was reading. I thought, *What's wrong with me? This stuff sounds like it's straight out of an evangelical publication. What am I missing? Why can't I spot the errors? Am I losing it?*"

His alarm melted away only when another friend explained that the WCG had undergone monumental theological reformation in the past several years. My friend could hardly believe it. Had the church *really* moved away from the aberrant and even heretical doctrinal positions that had marked it for so many years? Yes, he was told, it really had done so. All he could do was shake his head.

THE PROTESTANT CONNECTION

I think my friend would have shaken his head even more vigorously had he known that nearly all of the doctrinal distinctives that Herbert Armstrong taught originated not with him, but with *Protestant* groups (albeit extreme and even heretical ones).

Mr. Armstrong was nothing in his theological approach if not eclectic. He borrowed and adapted most of his "unique" teachings from others. Often when we try to tell some of our people that Mr. Armstrong borrowed much of his teaching from outside sources, we meet heavy resistance. So we sometimes respond with the following: "Allow us to lay out a challenge aimed at combatting the idea that these doctrines were specially revealed to Herbert Armstrong. We want to show that they really did not pour directly from the Godhead into his mind. Here's our challenge: You know the distinctive teachings of Herbert Armstrong; now you name the teaching and we'll tell you where it came from. We'll show you what preceded Herbert Armstrong and demonstrate that the teaching was *not* specially revealed to him and it *wasn't* restored from the first century."

When someone takes us up on this challenge, almost always the first doctrine to be mentioned is *the Sabbath.* "Sorry!" I say. "The Seventh-day Baptists had that first, long before Mr. Armstrong." You should see the looks on people's faces as we start naming the origins of one doctrine after another.

How about *the nature of man?* Sorry—the evangelist Charles Finney heavily influenced our former ideas on that. In fact, after Mr. Armstrong's death when my dad moved into his predecessor's office and cleaned out his desk, guess what book he found there explaining the nature of man? You guessed it—a work by Charles Finney.

Well, what about *Anglo-Israelism?* Certainly that one was specially revealed to Mr. Armstrong! Well, not exactly. A man named John Sadler apparently pioneered the idea way back in 1649, while another man named Richard Brothers (1757–1824) developed the concept further. It's true Mr. Armstrong took their ideas and adapted them in a peculiar way, but he emphatically *did not* originate the concept. In fact, it is no secret that Herbert Armstrong's *The United States and the British Commonwealth in Prophecy* was copied from a book titled *Judah's Scepter and Joseph's Birthright*[1] by J. H. Allen.

It is possible to run down almost the entire list of "new truths" supposedly revealed to Mr. Armstrong and point out where he got them and what preceded them. And most interesting of all (at least for me) is that most of these teachings he learned from Protestants. Contrary to what we formerly believed, none of our distinctive doctrines was specially revealed to Mr. Armstrong—at least not in the way the term "specially revealed" is commonly understood. And therein lies another story.

A STORY: MORE THAN A GRAIN OF TRUTH

A story which cannot be documented nevertheless gives an accurate understanding of how Mr. Armstrong used the term *revealed*. Before Mr. Armstrong moved to California, he and John Kiesz, a former Church of God (Seventh Day) minister who is now deceased, were working together in Eugene, Oregon. Mr. Armstrong was putting out initial copies of *The Plain Truth* and had started his radio broadcast. The men were sharing an office, and John Kiesz came in one day to find Mr. Armstrong pounding away on the typewriter.

"Herbert, what are you doing?" Mr. Kiesz asked.

"John," Mr. Armstrong replied, "God has revealed this incredible new truth to me." You must understand that in our former system, "new truth" was the ultimate find. When my parents first joined the church back in the fifties, I remember my mom and dad being asked one question repeatedly. The question wasn't, "How did you come to join the Worldwide Church of God?" but "When did you come into *The Truth*?" Not "When did you accept Christ?" but "When did you come into *The Truth*?" For us, new truth was the pearl of great price.

Back to the story. As John Kiesz peered over Mr. Armstrong's shoulder and looked at the article being typed, he recognized it. "Herbert," he said, "this appeared in *The Bible Advocate* [the Church of God (Seventh Day) magazine] about three months ago."

"Yes, that's how God revealed it to me," Mr. Armstrong enthusiastically replied.

This story, told to me by Mr. Kiesz himself, illustrates the fact that Mr. Armstrong used the term *revealed* in a way substantially different from how one might see it defined in most dictionaries or seminary textbooks. When he said something had been revealed to him, he did not mean that God had poured the new understanding directly into his waiting mind. No, whatever the new teaching happened to be, it usually came through a more human channel.

When some people hear this for the first time, they wrongly assume that Mr. Armstrong knowingly talked about "new revelation" in a deceitfully malicious way. When he'd talk about ideas being revealed to him, most people automatically assumed he meant revealed in the sense of Paul's experience on the Damascus road or Isaiah's experience when he was called into ministry as described in Isaiah 6. But this would be to misunderstand. Mr. Armstrong's use of the term *revealed* was a good deal more elastic than that, and I don't believe it was deliberately deceitful or malicious. Yet it did create a picture for people that God was somehow directly communicating new ideas and teachings to Mr. Armstrong through some kind of divine pipeline. That, of course, created all kinds of problems.

A STROLL THROUGH PAST HEADLINES

When people sincerely believe that their spiritual leader has the ultimate inside track on divine wisdom, they cannot help but sit up and take notice when he speaks—especially if what he says concerns their eternal welfare or destruction. Imagine for a moment that you were convinced your own pastor had a direct line from God, that what he said was the absolute truth, and that when he spoke, you had better listen and take heed. Imagine also that he made most of his pronouncements through a church newsletter. What would you think when you saw headlines like the following, knowing that they were directed to *you* from your undisputed spiritual leader?

HOW YOU DRESS FOR CHURCH—

Could it keep you out of the KINGDOM?[2]

How subtly Satan used MAKEUP to start the Church off the track[3]

OUR LIGHT IS SHINING!—and not the cosmetics on our faces[4]

My guess is you'd probably respond a lot like we did—with firm dedication laced with fear. Our spiritual lives were heavy with rules and threats. Most of us began to measure ourselves more by what we didn't do than by what we did. As our rule books grew thick, our concept of grace grew correspondingly thin. We did not so much have a vital relationship with Christ as we had a cognitive acceptance of certain esoteric doctrines. *Who* you knew wasn't nearly so important as *what* you knew. Doctrine—new truth—was everything to us. It's what set us apart from everyone else. And my, did it set us apart!

SEVEN KEY DOCTRINAL EMPHASES

For those who may not be familiar with what the Worldwide Church of God formerly taught, allow me to briefly sketch out seven areas of doctrine that, taken together, set us apart from all other organizations, denominations, and churches. Our former doctrinal distinctives cannot be limited to the following, but in my opinion what follows represents the chief teachings that defined us as a group and distinguished us from all others. *Please* remember: The Worldwide Church of God no longer holds to, teaches, or defends any of these doctrines. What I am about to describe is the former doctrinal edifice of the Worldwide Church of God. In large part, the following description will apply to the vast majority of our splinter groups. (For a brief comparison of what the church formerly taught with what it teaches today, see the appendix.)

1. Who Is God?

While the Worldwide Church of God has always taught that God was eternal, immutable, and sovereign, it also used to teach that He was constantly learning and growing. We taught that God the Father had a human form, as we do. Consider this:

Now notice once again Genesis 1:26: "...God (Elohim) said, Let us make man in our image, after our likeness [form and shape]..." God is described in the Bible as having eyes, ears, nose, mouth—hair on his head—arms, legs, fingers, toes. Jesus was "…the express image of his [the Father's] Person…" (Hebrews 1:3).[5]

From this passage you see that our God was not entirely orthodox. He had eyes, ears, nose, mouth—all the bodily parts we have. On the one hand, we were right in saying the Bible used these words to describe Him; the Psalms, for example, are full of such terms in reference to God. On the other hand, we can now see, by God's grace, that these terms are used anthropomorphically, to picture God in a poetic way. I think we understood this principle a little even then, for we never did take all such terms literally. We never taught, for example, that God had feathers, as a woodenly literal reading of Psalm 17:8 would require, nor that He sometimes acted like a drunk, as Psalm 78:65 would suggest. That was too literal even for us.

Our heretical concept of God did not stop there. We vigorously denied the Trinity, claiming that it was a pagan doctrine. Although we upheld the deity of Christ, we understood Him to be a *separate* God from the Father; while we said He had always existed with God Almighty, we also taught He did not become the Son of God until He was born into the world through the virgin Mary. And the Holy Spirit? We denied His personality and taught that "He" was really an "it," as the following passage shows:

> If the Holy Spirit is not a Person—a Ghost—then what does the Bible reveal about the Holy Spirit?… The Holy Spirit is the Spirit (not Ghost) that emanates out from both God and Christ everywhere in the universe. Through His Holy Spirit, God projects Himself, in Spirit, everywhere in the universe—yet both God and Christ have form and shape, even as man.
>
> The Holy Spirit is many things. It is the VERY LIFE of the immortal God, which, entering in a human, begets him with GOD-life.
>
> It is the POWER of God, by which, when Christ "spake" it was

done. It is the POWER by which God stretched out the heavens—created the vast endless universe.

The Holy Spirit, entering into man as God's gift, opens the mind to UNDERSTANDING of spiritual knowledge, unknown to the human mind otherwise. It is the LOVE of God "…shed abroad in our hearts…" (Romans 5:5). It is the FAITH of Christ, which may be given to God's begotten children through the Holy Spirit. It is the POWER of God, begotten within humans, enabling us to overcome Satan and sin.[6]

We taught that the primary mission of Jesus was to prove that the law could be kept. We said that the Holy Spirit came to the believer to implant the life and character of Jesus. In that way we were able to obey the commandments of God.

Finally, we taught that the destiny of all true believers (that is, members in good standing of the WCG) was to become God even as God is God. We said that we would become part of a "God family." The quest of every believer was to become God even as He is God. This is one reason we so vigorously attacked the doctrine of the Trinity. In our minds, the Trinity limited God to three Persons—hardly an acceptable teaching when you insisted that every believer's destiny was to become a literal God in the God family. We put it like this:

> Emperor Constantine of the Roman Empire government called the Nicene Council in A.D. 325 and made both, the pagan Easter (from the goddess Astarte) and the Trinity doctrine, LAW!… The Trinity doctrine *limited* God to three Persons.[7]

These days, of course, we have admitted our error and have embraced the biblical and orthodox doctrine of the Trinity: one God existing eternally as three coequal, divine Persons. We believe that God is spirit and therefore does not have bodily parts as we do, and that Jesus' primary mission was to seek and to save that which was lost (we humans!). The Holy Spirit does empower us to live godly lives but not as a mere "force" or "energy."

2. Who Is Man?

While we thought that true believers would be resurrected to eternal life, we taught that unbelievers remained dead for one thousand years longer. This would have major implications for our teaching on the afterlife.

We taught that God was literally reproducing Himself through mankind. Our destiny was not to remain merely human, but to become God—born again as members of God's family. Just as human children are fully human, so (we thought) God's children will be fully God.

Today we recognize that our destiny is not to become God; He is forever separate, holy, and blessed, "the blessed and only Ruler, the King of kings and Lord of lords, who alone is immortal and who lives in unapproachable light, whom no one has seen or can see" (1 Timothy 6:15–16). He alone is uncreated; we are His creation, brought into existence by His creative power. He is without beginning or ending. We humans have a beginning. The redeemed will one day be glorified and receive indestructible bodies like that of the Lord Jesus after His resurrection, but we will never become God. That is impossible.

3. What Is Salvation?

We used to teach that no one was "born again" until the final resurrection. We said that those who believed in the death and resurrection of Jesus and who committed themselves to obeying the law were "begotten" (which we understood to mean "conceived") sons of God and would be "born again" at the time of the resurrection. Until then, a believer was only conceived, not born. Therefore, no one was "saved" in their earthly life; they had to await the return of Jesus Christ for that. At the resurrection the believer would be raised up and finally be born again. "We are begotten sons of God if we have the Holy Spirit. And therefore, we are impregnated with immortal life, to have it when Christ comes, which will be in the Family of God."[8]

This was one of the few doctrines taught by Mr. Armstrong that has no known precedent; it appears to be unique to him. He developed this teaching through a simple misunderstanding of the original Greek text underlying the New Testament. He erroneously claimed that the Greek word *gennao* ("beget," KJV) was the only word used for this activity in the New Testament. Yet at least three other terms—*apokueo, anagennao, tikto*—are used interchangeably with *gennao* and can be translated "conceive," "bring forth," "deliver," etc. Experts in the Greek language—as well as a properly utilized lexicon—can easily point out the correct understanding of this term. First Peter 1:23 makes it clear that our former understanding was in error: "For you *have been* born again, not of perishable seed, but of imperishable, through the living and enduring word of God" (emphasis mine).

We also claimed that while Christ died for the sins of the world, believing in Christ was insufficient to gain salvation; the believer must also obey Christ. That obedience, as we formerly understood it, included adherance to the Saturday Sabbath, to dietary laws (as in Leviticus 11), and observance of religious festivals, new moons, and holy days. We taught that only those who obeyed all the commandments—including those portions of the Old Covenant law that Herbert Armstrong believed and taught to "still be in effect"—could achieve salvation. In other words, while salvation was a gift, one had to qualify to receive this free gift. Adam had to qualify to restore the government of God on earth; he failed. Christ had to qualify by overcoming Satan and proving loyal to God and God's way; He succeeded. In the same way, each one in the church also had to "qualify" in order to sit on Christ's throne with Him. It was a sort of conditional grace, which helps to explain how Mr. Armstrong could make such statements as, "Jesus Christ does not make it EASY for any of us whom God calls and Jesus uses in His service— or those called for salvation. To qualify for the free GIFT of salvation is not easy."[9]

Today we teach that people are born again the moment they put their trust in the living Savior, Jesus Christ. Salvation is a gift and cannot be earned or "qualified for" in any way: "For it is by grace you have been saved, through faith—and this not from yourselves, it is the gift of God—not by works, so that no one can boast" (Ephesians 2:8).

4. What Is the Church?

We were adamant that God had only one true church in the world, and we were it. All others were false and apostate. We labeled Roman Catholicism "the Great Whore of Babylon" (from Revelation 17) and called Protestants her harlot daughters.

Herbert Armstrong also claimed that the true gospel ceased to be preached from about A.D. 53 when it was squelched by the Great Whore. The truth reappeared nineteen centuries later under the leadership of Mr. Armstrong. He was Christ's apostle in the last days who would restore lost truth to the church in order to prepare for Christ's imminent Second Coming.

How did we know we were the "only true church"? For one thing, we had the "correct" name, "the church of God." We were known as the "Radio Church of God," until 1968 when we changed our name to the Worldwide Church of God. Second, we observed God's Sabbath, along with the Old Covenant dietary laws and special feast days. We required the celebration of seven annual Sabbaths (Leviticus 23)—one of which lasted for eight days—and avoided pork, shrimp, and certain other meats. The WCG interpreted the Bible to discourage members from voting, to prohibit righteous people from serving in the military, marrying after being divorced, relying on doctors (for anything other than accidents, "repair surgery" or childcare), using cosmetics, or observing Christmas, Easter, and birthdays. No other church followed all these strict practices; therefore, they were apostate and we were righteous.

Because this was true, we distanced ourselves from every other "Christian falsely so-called" and all other denominations. We became isolated and set apart. Information about the time and location of services was carefully guarded. Prospective members were carefully screened and invited to services only when they "were almost ready for baptism."[10] We saw ourselves as God's only true church and we didn't hide our belief. A headline from a *Good News* published on December 18, 1978, blares, "THE WORLDWIDE CHURCH OF GOD *TODAY*" and is subheaded, "the only voice in the wilderness of today's religious Babylon giving a hopeless world its ONLY and SURE HOPE!"[11]

And what of the organization of God's one true church? In the beginning, we were organized in a largely democratic fashion. In a six-thousand-word article written in 1939 and titled "Did Christ Reorganize the Church?" Herbert Armstrong thoroughly condemned centralized, hierarchical church government, and enthusiastically supported congregational autonomy. He wrote, "All authority and power to rule is limited solely to each LOCAL congregation. But there is NO BIBLE AUTHORITY for any super-government, or organization with authority over the local congregations!" He blamed Emperor Constantine for instituting a hierarchical system, as he had blamed him for introducing the doctrine of the Trinity.

Yet over time the WCG itself would institute a rigid hierarchical system. On January 22, 1955, Mr. Armstrong said that "for the first time in 750 years God's complete government is restored to His Church." On that day, he said, every administrative office mentioned in Scripture had been recognized and filled in the Radio Church of God—apostle, evangelist, pastor, minister-elder (preaching elder), deacon, and deaconess. By the midfifties it could be said that "the congregations are ruled by the elders, who are ruled by the evangelists, and they are ruled by the apostle who is ruled by Christ who is ruled by God. All offices are appointed, by a superior office. It is government from God down to each individual member of the church."[12]

Other things would change in "God's church," as well. Mr. Armstrong was not always called "Christ's apostle." But by the early 1950s some students at Ambassador began to refer to him that way. Soon others picked it up. The first time he was publicly called an apostle was in 1951 at a Feast of Tabernacles, when Herman Hoeh, one of the first graduates of Ambassador College and ministers of the church, used the title in a sermon. Mr. Armstrong later wrote, "At that time his words hit my startled ears like an atomic bomb and my first impulse was to deny and correct his statement immediately."[13] In 1955 he acknowledged the truth of this title, but he rarely used it or even mentioned it for the next twenty years. When he did use it, he would call himself "the one you [ministers and others] call an apostle." By the seventies he had begun to use the term frequently, and in the last decade of his life he often called himself "the sole apostle of the twentieth century."

Today we reject what is well known as "Armstrongism," that is, adherence to the teachings of Herbert W. Armstrong in lieu of biblical evidence to the contrary. We have accepted the primacy of the Bible and of the gospel, while more than one hundred splinter groups that the WCG spawned continue to teach and proclaim the unbiblical interpretations of a man. We do not believe the WCG is God's only true church; we know there are genuine believers in all Christian denominations. We do not believe that one form of church government is more biblical than another and are taking steps to decentralize our ecclesiastical structure. God's church has continued to thrive through all of the centuries since Jesus rose from the grave two millennia ago; we are simply one small part of the Bride of Christ. And we are happy to be so!

5. How Should We Handle the Old Covenant?

This question shaped a multitude of beliefs and practices in our church. The New Covenant/Old Covenant debate is a significant piece of the puzzle because a mixed understanding of this existed in our church for a long time. Many people thought we were still under the Old Covenant, primarily because many of our ministers were teaching exactly that.

I remember Ted Armstrong giving a sermon in Pasadena about this topic. He asked the audience, "How many people here think we're under the New Covenant? Raise your hand." Scores of hands went up. Then he asked, "And how many people think we're under the Old Covenant? Raise your hand." More hands went up. Then he said, "By the time I'm done this morning, you'll know what kind of a church we are."

Then he took us on a tour of scores of verses, highlighting the word *commandments* wherever it appeared (out of context, of course, but we were all ignorant of that). His concluding verse was Hebrews 8:13, which says, "In that he saith, A new covenant, he hath made the first old. Now that which decayeth and waxeth old is ready to vanish away" (KJV). He fixed on that final phrase and said, "See, it hasn't yet vanished away. It waxeth old, but it's still in force; it hasn't vanished."

As we sat there listening to him deliver this sermon, we were biblically ignorant. We had no idea that the Book of Hebrews was written just a few years before the destruction of the Jewish temple in A.D. 70. When the invading Roman army razed the temple and burned Jerusalem to the ground, the old mode of relating to God was certainly done away with, forever. The Roman legions of Titus saw to it that the Old Covenant system "vanished" once and for all. Yet almost two thousand years after those events had occurred, we remained firmly convinced by Ted's presentation that we were still under the Old Covenant.

Even so, the question didn't stay settled for long. Troubling objections continued to be raised. How could we still be under the Old Covenant when we never made any of the animal sacrifices that were at the heart of that covenant? And how could we say that Christ did away with that aspect of the covenant, but the rest of it was still intact and in force? How did one decide which portions of the Old Covenant still applied and which ones didn't?

In 1978 Herbert Armstrong wrote an article intended to clear up the confusion.[14] He wrote that while it was correct to say we were no longer under the Old Covenant, yet we were not yet under the New Covenant either; that wouldn't begin until Christ returned. So where were we? We were "between" the two covenants.

Such a pronouncement gave Mr. Armstrong a platform from which to pick and choose which items from the Old Covenant and which items from the New would apply to us. It explains how we could be required to observe Old Covenant holy days but not be required to make animal sacrifices for sin. Whatever we were commanded to obey, however, we were commanded to obey in no uncertain terms.

By God's grace, we have left all this behind. We are not an Old Covenant church, but a New Covenant church. We do not earn our standing before God by doing anything (although what we do certainly reveals what is in our heart). We live by grace, not by law; by the New Covenant, not the Old.

6. What Is a True View of History?

One of Mr. Armstrong's chief teachings was his own version of British-Israelism. He taught that the Anglo-Saxons (the British peoples) are direct descendants of the ten "lost" tribes of Israel. He said the ten tribes of Israel migrated to north-western Europe and are to be found today primarily in England and the English-speaking world. The Anglo-Saxons of England and the United States, he said, are the descendants of Ephraim and Manasseh.

How did he come to this conclusion? Tortured etymology gives one answer. For example, he said that the Hebrew word for "covenant" (*berith*) became significant in English when combined with the Hebrew word for "man" (*ish*). Since vowels are not written in the Masoretic text of the original Hebrew text, the *e* in *berith* drops out to form the term *brith*. Since ancient Hebrews did not pronounce the *h*, *berith* became *brit*. Put that together with *ish* and you have "British." Of course, there are no biblical or historical reasons to make such leaps in logic.

He did something similar with the term "Saxon." Genesis 21:12 tells us that God promised to bless Isaac's seed. If the *I* in Isaac is dropped, we are left with *saac*—and it is "Saac's sons" (*Saxon*) with whom God's covenant was established. Therefore when Jesus said He had been sent only to "the lost sheep of Israel," He meant He had come to deliver His message not to the Jews, but to the Anglo-Saxon people. Mr. Armstrong wrote, "Jesus had told His disciples to go NOT to the gentiles, but to the 'lost sheep of the House of Israel.' The 'House of Israel' *never* refers to the Jews—always to the kingdom that became known as 'the lost ten tribes.' They were in Western Europe and Britain when Jesus gave this instruction."[15] Earlier he had insisted: "So here is another TRUTH unknown in the teachings of most churches called Christianity—Israel was divided into TWO nations—and the people of the kingdom of Israel *were NOT Jews,* nor are they ever called Jews in the Bible!"[16]

At other times he would claim that the current English throne is an extension of the throne of David and that the Stone of Scone, which used to lie beneath the royal English throne, is actually the very rock Jacob used for a pillow as described in Genesis 28:11. Mr. Armstrong claimed the stone had been transported by the prophet Jeremiah to the British isles (yet geologists say the stone is calcareous, a type common to Scotland, and is inconsistent with rocks from Palestine). In many ways this doctrine of British-Israelism shaped our major beliefs and practices.

Beyond British-Israelism, we were taught false church history. It was commonly maintained, for example, that the man often referred to as Simon Magus (Acts 8:9–25) started the Roman Catholic Church—a claim which is simply wrong. Such false history shaped much of what we did and taught.

Sometimes we would be directed to a diagram of church history. It would indicate the beginning of the church at Pentecost at one end of the diagram and where we were in the twentieth century. In between was little good. The gospel had ceased to be proclaimed in A.D. 53; a little while later the "church" abandoned the Sabbath and replaced it with Sunday-keeping. This is where the church got off track.

So according to the diagram, the church started well, then almost immediately got on a descending line until finally it was corrupt. Still, the church never completely lost sight of all the truth. Through time a number of remnant people—the Waldensians, the Bogomils, the Lollards—were persecuted by the Great Whore. We preached and taught that these people were true Christians. Why? Regardless of what else they may have believed or practiced, they were true Christians because they had the "Sabbath truth."

It's interesting for us today to look at some of these groups honestly. Many of them were gnostics and deists. Waldensians were Trinitarians and were not Sabbath keepers; they kept Sunday as their Sabbath. But because they used the word "Sabbath" in their writings, we mistakenly assumed they worshiped on Saturday. At some point a few Waldensians did break off from the main group and started keeping Saturday as the Sabbath, but the majority of the church never did so.

We absolutely accepted this deeply flawed version of history. In truth, there's something appealing even to the Protestant mind about such a view of history. We know the Roman Church *did* wander off track through its medieval teachings of indulgences and its general corruption. We know that Martin Luther *did* a great thing by igniting the flame of the Reformation. There's something good about such a view of history—but there's something troubling about it, too, even beyond the wild inaccuracies. We saw conspiracy everywhere, a parallel track of good and evil. The groups that "had the Sabbath truth"or the ones we thought had the Sabbath) were good; the others were corrupt because they didn't have the Sabbath. Everything for us was colored by this skewed view of history.

7. What Does the Future Hold?

In our former view, all of history looked to the millennium as the pinnacle of righteousness and godliness. Christ would come back to set up His government and reign for a thousand years, and we would be His partners. All that He did on earth at His first advent—His sinless life, His sacrificial death, and His resurrection from the grave—were nothing but preliminaries to the kingdom. He came not so much to save us from our sins (although He did that) as to proclaim and lay the groundwork for the coming kingdom of God.

At the resurrection and the beginning of the millennium, dead believers would be resurrected and born again to reign with Christ on the earth. As Herbert Armstrong wrote: "The KINGDOM OF GOD is a literal GOVERNMENT. Even as the Chaldean Empire was a KINGDOM—even as the Roman Empire was a KINGDOM—so the KINGDOM OF GOD is a government. It is to *take over* the GOVERNMENT of the NATIONS of the world."[17]

And when would this cataclysmic event happen? Mr. Armstrong taught that it could happen at any time and offered many predictions about its timing (all of which failed to come true). He said that the Worldwide Church of God would first be miraculously transported to a place of safety, probably Petra—an ancient, walled city in the south of Jordan, a place of protection against the terrors of Armageddon—in 1936. He later mistakenly predicted that this event would occur in '43 and then again in '72. Three and a half years after the church was taken to safety, Christ would return and the battle of Armageddon would commence. When all these predictions failed and numbers of people left the church in response, he became much more careful about setting prophetic dates.

Finally, we taught there were three separate resurrections:

1. Members of the true church, as well as departed saints, would be raised to life to meet the returning Christ and establish the millennial kingdom. At that time they would be born again and become literal Gods in the "God Family."

2. Those who had not heard "the Truth" in their lifetime would be resurrected at the end of the millennium, at which time the saints would teach them correct doctrine. If they refused to accept it, there was only one fate.

3. Willful sinners were to be resurrected from the dead, only to be thrown into the lake of fire, where they would perish and cease to exist for eternity.

Today we no longer hold this three-resurrection eschatological scheme to be a test of fellowship. We recognize that true Christians can and do differ on their views of future things; this does not make them less Christian or spiritually inferior. Our members vary in their beliefs about eschatological details. But we all believe that Christ will return one day in power and great glory and that "he must reign until he has put all his enemies under his feet. The last enemy to be destroyed is death" (1 Corinthians 15:25–26). We believe God to be fair, just, and merciful. We look forward to spending eternity with Christ and all the saints, not as fellow-Gods, but as glorified chidren of God—redeemed men and women who love Him and will worship Him forever.

A MASTER SALESMAN

As I mentioned in the last chapter, before Mr. Armstrong entered the ministry, he was an advertising man and salesman. He did a wonderful job in those roles; many experts called him one of the great copywriters of the twentieth century, and we admire him for that.

Unfortunately, he brought that sales mentality into the founding of our church. It appears that he said to himself, "All right, I've got to make this church different. How do I make people want to come to this church and not some other church?"

Many of our members still ask this question sixty years later: "How are we different anymore? In the old days we always were different. What sets us apart today?" One of Herbert Armstrong's greatest successes was in making us different; we thought nobody else had the Truth but us.

Think of it like this. Suppose you start to market a new brand of soap. So you say to yourself, "OK, I'm selling soap. I've got to distinguish my soap from Tide and from Ivory and from all the others. So what do I do?

"For one, I can start positioning my product by identifying all others as inferior or even worthless, as misleading, as spurious and even hurtful. Of course, I will have to use basically the same ingredients for my soap that they do in theirs, but I will change the name of those ingredients. It'll be basically the same thing, but I'll give it a slightly different name."

I don't think that this really went though Mr. Armstrong's head, but in fact it is what happened. We were told that we were the "only true" soap. So when we started admitting a few years ago that we *weren't* the only true soap, that others had been making excellent soap for centuries, what do you think some of our people did? Many of them left. But where could they go? They would never use the mainline soap. They would never become an evangelical Christian—why, that soap was falsely so-called, it was heretical, it was bogus. So what could they do? In their disillusionment many of them started spinning off to splinter groups.

THE EMERGENCE OF SPLINTER GROUPS

We started making doctrinal changes in 1987, but a number of splits occurred before that—thirty-four, actually. Fourteen of those thirty-four are splits of splits. The names of these groups are revealing: The Plainer Truth; the Mystery Church of God; the Mystery of the Kingdom Ministry; and my all-time favorite, the New Moon, the Church of God in the Netherlands.

Many of these groups are still meeting, although the numbers in each are small. Some have rather tragic stories. A year after The Family Church of God began, for example, the leader and his wife divorced. Our largest splinter group, the United Church of God, formed shortly after my dad gave the 1994 Christmas Eve sermon (see chapter 7). It has about eighteen thousand members. The Global Church of God counts about seven thousand members and is led by one of Mr. Armstrong's first students, Roderick Meredith. The Church of God, Philadelphia era, is the oldest of these major splits and has about three thousand members.

A minority of our former members—it would be hard to assign a number—have joined other Christian denominations. These people may have felt the WCG congregation they were attending wasn't making changes fast enough. Or they may have been dissatisfied with their pastor. Or perhaps they had significant numbers of family members in other denominations. Others simply have found that their local WCG congregation was not equipped for fully serving the needs of all members, in light of the many changes we made. They felt they needed to go elsewhere in the Body of Christ to find help and healing. We are not happy to lose those people, but we are glad they're joining a healthy, Bible-believing, authentic church.

So after all the doctrinal changes of the past few years, here's where we stand: Close to seventy thousand people remain with us, which means that we have lost about seventy thousand members. Only thirty thousand people, perhaps less than that, attend the splinter groups. A larger group of forty thousand people sit at home, confused, frustrated, and not knowing what to do or what to believe. So they go nowhere; they're dropping out of everything.

My earnest hope is that all will be led by the Spirit of God to embrace the real gospel of the Living Savior and will find the abundant life He promises to give. That abundant life doesn't come in accepting a bushelful of esoteric doctrine but in coming humbly to the Author of Life Himself, Jesus Christ. He and no other is the center and focus of the gospel. I cannot end this chapter any better than with the words of the apostle John at the close of the final book in the New Testament: "The Spirit and the bride say, 'Come!' And let him who hears say, 'Come!' Whoever is thirsty, let him come; and whoever wishes, let him take the free gift of the water of life" (Revelation 22:17).

CHAPTER EIGHT

THE FIRST REFORMS

Not long before he died, Herbert Armstrong told my dad that some things in the church needed to be changed. He didn't make a list of the changes he had in mind, he simply said that "things needed to be changed."

What things might he have intended? We can never be sure—with one notable exception. Near the end of his life, Mr. Armstrong said that our stance on divine healing needed change.

FAITH + OBEDIENCE = HEALING

At least as far back as 1952, when he published *Does God Heal Today?*, Mr. Armstrong was teaching that it was always God's will to heal His obedient, faithful children. He begins that early work by quoting Exodus 15:23–26 (KJV) calling it a report of "the first account in all history of direct divine healing."[1] He calls special attention to the last part of that passage:

> If thou wilt diligently hearken unto the voice of the LORD thy God, and wilt do that which is right in His sight, and wilt give ear to His commandments, and keep all His statutes, I will put none of these diseases upon thee, which I have brought upon the Egyptians: for *I am the LORD that healeth thee.*
>
> And do you know, that the same conditions, "If you will obey and keep my commandments," etc.—apply today, and that's one reason why

a lot of people who have a little light on divine healing and believe in it are not being healed![2]

From there Mr. Armstrong moved on to claim that anyone seeking to be healed in any way other than direct divine healing was guilty of idolatry. He also taught that Scripture condemns medicine as idolatry, that the origins of medicine could be found in paganism, and that modern people had ignored this truth to their own hurt:

> So many seem to believe we should go to the doctors, they pray for God to cause their medicines to heal. They assume God raised up medical science and blesses it and works through it. But this is merely the same old Pagan practice of idolatry though very few realize it today. Truly all nations have been DECEIVED into practicing Pagan idolatry believing it is true Christianity! For the real Christian who has faith in God there is a better way.[3]

And what was that better way? Pure and simple, it was faith. His teaching was based on interpretations of passages such as James 5:14–15, Isaiah 53:4–5, Matthew 9:2, 1 Peter 2:24, Exodus 15:26, and Psalm 103:3. If someone had faith in God, he didn't need doctors. After all, since healing is nothing but forgiveness of sin, and Christ died to pay the penalty for sin, then the way to get healed is to put one's faith in the Healer and in no one and nothing else.

Mr. Armstrong also made a big distinction between physical sin and spiritual sin, a distinction he continued until he died. He said that Christ's physical beating before he was crucified paid the penalty for physical sin (and thereby paved the way for our physical healing), while his death on the cross paid the penalty for spiritual sin (and thereby paved the way for us to receive eternal life). Here is how he developed this unusual dichotomy:

> Now God "forgiveth ALL thine inquities," and "healeth ALL thy diseases."

Well, *how* does God forgive our spiritual sins? Sin is the transgression of LAW (I John 3:4). That's the Bible definition of SIN. God's law of "LOVE" is a *spiritual* law (Rom. 7:14). The penalty is DEATH (Rom. 6:23). HOW does God forgive our spiritual transgressions—remove the DEATH penalty from us? Why, by having *given* His only begotten Son, who, while we were yet sinners, DIED FOR US (John 3:16; Rom. 5:8). In other words, CHRIST PAID THE PENALTY IN OUR STEAD! So, since He paid the penalty we incurred, for us, in our stead, God legally can remove the penalty from us. We do not have to pay the penalty, *because* JESUS *paid it for us!*

Then HOW does God forgive *physical* sins? Why, exactly the same way! Jesus paid the penalty of them, too, in our stead! Is that in the Scripture? Most certainly it is!

Here it is: "(Jesus) healed ALL that were sick, That it might be fulfilled which was spoken by Isaiah the prophet, saying, *'Himself took our infirmities, and bare our sicknesses'* (Matt. 8:16–17)."

There it is! Turn to it in your own Bible, and read it! Jesus healed ALL that were sick, because He, Himself took our physical infirmities and bare our sicknesses!

And HOW?

Let Peter answer: *By His STRIPES,* ye are healed—I Peter 2:24!

Just before Jesus was taken out to be crucified, He submitted voluntarily to being BEATEN WITH STRIPES. "Then released he Barabbas unto them: and when he had *scourged Jesus,* he delivered Him to be crucified" (Matt. 27:26). "Then Pilate…took Jesus, and *scourged Him"* (John 19:1). Jesus suffered this PHYSICAL PAIN, actually breaking open His body in great welts, in order to pay *for you,* in your stead, the pain, suffering, sickness, or other penalty of your physical transgressions![4]

With that doctrinal groundwork laid, Mr. Armstrong believed that real Christians do not run to doctors for healing, but to God. If a member were to go to a doctor, he would be disregarding the scourging of Christ's passion. The only legitimate role for doctors, in Mr. Armstrong's opinion, was "to help you to observe nature's laws by prescribing correct diet, teaching you how better to live according to nature's laws. In other words, to PREVENT sickness, not heal after you are sick![5] Doctors might also be legitimately called upon in special cases, Mr. Armstrong wrote, such as in childbearing or to set a broken bone. But in the vast majority of cases:

> Here's God's instruction to YOU, today, if you are ill. If we are to live by every Word of God, we should obey this Scripture. God does not say call your family physician. Instead, notice:
>
> "Is any sick among you? *let him call for the elders of the church;* and let them PRAY over him anointing him with oil in the name of the Lord; *and the prayer of* FAITH *shall save the sick,* and the Lord shall raise him up; and if he have committed sins, they shall be forgiven him" (James 5:14–15).
>
> He does not say, call the doctors and let them give medicines and drugs, and God will cause the medicines and drugs and dope to cure you.... Instead God says call GOD'S MINISTERS. And let them PRAY, anointing with oil (the type and symbol of the Holy Spirit). Then GOD PROMISES He will HEAL YOU![6]

Mr. Armstrong maintained this position for most of his life. A later booklet called *The Plain Truth about Healing,* published in 1979, expanded on his earlier ideas without changing their basic premise. His teaching still could be summed up like this: "The very fact that two *conditions* to miraculous healing by God are obedience and faith *requires* the exercise of, and therefore GROWTH in, obedience and faith."[7]

Yet, Mr. Armstrong already seemed to be making room for the idea that not all those who lived in faith and obedience would be physically healed in this life:

A minister, apparently lacking either in faith or in UNDERSTANDING, writes, "Case histories in the Bible, and especially thousands of case histories in the present Church, show that faith was present in the lives of people, and God did not heal."

I could not vouch for the fact that FAITH was present in all such cases—I cannot judge others; only God can. The same letter gives the following, striking home to me, in contending against God's PROMISES to heal on faith: "What about the many of our dead we have buried— Mrs. Loma Armstrong [the wife of my youth who died at age 75½], your son Dick…" and four others.

My answer, in simple FAITH, is that they, like Abraham, Isaac and Jacob, all died in FAITH, not having received the PROMISES—*YET!* But in the next fraction of a second from their loss of consciousness in death, THEY SHALL WAKE UP *HEALED*—in the resurrection, and in GOD'S KINGDOM! I have *faith* that in the not-too-distant future I shall SEE my father, my first wife, my son Dick and others this minister named FULLY *HEALED* in the Kingdom of God.[8]

In this same booklet, Mr. Armstrong also made it clear that visiting a doctor was not just cause for being disfellowshiped; he said the church did not condemn a member who used the medical profession.

God's Church does not judge or condemn those who, through lack of faith, utilize the services of the medical profession. God's Church merely says to you, HEALING IS INCLUDED—Christ already has PAID for it— it is a PROMISE of God (with conditions of obedience and faith) and it is one of God's BENEFITS that is *INCLUDED* in the gift of His grace!…

Notice, HEALING is one of the BENEFITS God gives us along with salvation. Like the meals on the steamship, IT IS INCLUDED—no extra charge. Jesus already PAID FOR IT! And God wants His people to learn to *rely on Him!*[9]

This teaching on divine healing remained in force and unchallenged until the last few years of Mr. Armstrong's life. With old age, of course, our bodies usually start to fail. The same was true of Mr. Armstrong, who lived to the ripe old age of ninety-three.

CHANGES IN THE WIND

In the last years of his life, Herbert Armstrong took a number of heart medications and had a full-time nurse travel with him everywhere he went. He used the medical profession for almost everything.

What amazes me now about this is that he would almost brag about what he was doing. He would write letters to the membership saying things like, "You know, most people can hardly get a doctor to visit their home, but I have two doctors who come to visit me on a regular basis." I found that many of our people were actually entertained by his admission. The tension between Mr. Armstrong's practice and his teaching almost never registered among some of us. Some of our braver people would come to ministers and pastors and ask quietly, "Is Mr. Armstrong *really* going to a doctor?" And we would tell them, "Yes, he's telling the truth!"

In the days before he died, this conflict finally began to sink in, especially with Mr. Armstrong himself. My dad asked him, "How could you take this medication? You're the one who wrote the booklet that insists God's people have no need of a doctor if only they obey and have sufficient faith. So how can you be using the medical profession? How do you want me to answer this question that church members are asking?"

The situation was made worse by the way some of our pastors responded to members who *did* go to doctors for help. Even when members were diagnosed with some catastrophic illness, their pastors might say to them, "The Bible teaches that going to a doctor shows a lack of faith!" Thankfully, most of our pastors were *not* that inflexible and judgmental—but far too many were.

All of these things finally conspired, I think, to make Herbert Armstrong realize that his stance toward the medical profession had to change. His conversation with my dad about this topic took place in 1985. By the end of January 1986, Mr. Armstrong was dead.

THE CHANGE BEGINS

One of the main problems with our doctrine on healing was its deficient view of faith. Not only did we teach that people of vibrant faith could ward off disease and sickness, we also taught that faith was the key to financial prosperity. We had bought into both of those doctrines, largely through the same sources that influence today's prosperity theology and faith movement. Not only did we believe that if a person did what God says, he would be materially blessed with higher salaries and better jobs—that was one example of how our flirtation with the covenant of blessing and cursing in Deuteronomy 27–28 worked its way out— but we also taught that if a person didn't do the right thing, he would be accursed. In other words, he would get sick. So if something's wrong and you can't figure it out, it must be caused by a secret sin. Of course, the guilt that accompanies such a flawed system can be absolutely devastating.

A whole year after Herbert Armstrong's death, a change was announced. My dad had asked several of us to start studying this question, and after a short time we all realized it was simply wrong to say that people suffered from inferior faith if they used doctors. It was wrong to say that using the medical profession demonstrated a lack of faith. We began to see that the whole health-and-wealth approach to the gospel was bogus and mistaken.

Once my dad was satisfied that we had studied the issue in enough depth to correct our old doctrinal stance, he decided to announce the church's new position in the March 23, 1987, edition of *The Worldwide News*. In an article titled "New Understanding of the Meaning of Christ's Broken Body and the Church's Teaching on HEALING," my father began a new era in the church when he wrote:

Now, I want to clarify some matters regarding the very important subject of *divine healing!*

Brethren, God has led me to see that the Church has misunderstood the concept of what we have called "physical sin." Let me now explain to you how we came to believe that physical illness was the result of "physical sin," and why the living and powerful Jesus Christ now leads me to clarify the Church's teaching on this misunderstood subject....

But now God has added a *new dimension* in understanding the transcendent purpose of Jesus' broken body. And as I stated earlier, Mr. Armstrong himself would have been the first one to *change* and accept new understanding when God made it clear.[10]

My father then went on to describe what this new understanding entailed. Among other things, he dealt with one of the chief passages Mr. Armstrong had used in his doctrine of divine healing, Psalm 103:2–3. In the King James Version, that text says, "Bless the LORD, O my soul, and forget not all his benefits: Who forgiveth all thine iniquities; who healeth all thy diseases." My father wrote about this passage:

In Psalm 103:2–3, healing "all thy diseases" is described as one of God's benefits. It is something, along with renewing our strength like the eagle's (verse 5), and executing "righteousness and judgment for all that are oppressed" (verse 6), that God grants as direct blessings and benefits that it is His *good pleasure* to give to those who serve and obey Him. But these are NOT *unconditional* promises that God is *bound* to give *in all circumstances for everyone!*

God knows our hearts and minds. He knows what is *best for us*. He knows what blessings to give and what blessings to withhold for our ultimate GOOD! But not *everyone's* strength is renewed like the eagle's now in this life. Nor has *every* righteous person received justice from oppression in his or her physical lifetime. In the same manner, while God can and *does* heal, and it is His desire and *will* to do so, He who sees all things KNOWS whether it is for the best in each circumstance or not.

Sometimes God heals one person as a witness or encouragement for others, perhaps even more so than for the sick person himself. The point is, in EVERY SITUATION *God knows what He is doing.* He is all-wise, all-powerful *and all-merciful!* He will not withhold a good thing from a person if it is truly in the best interests of all for that person to receive it.[11]

Further, my father insisted that whether someone is divinely healed is no evidence of his spiritual health (or lack of it). The prophet Elisha, he reminded his readers, was a faithful servant of God who died of an illness. The apostle Paul asked three times to be healed of a "thorn in the flesh" but was refused. Yet Scripture sees neither man as either disobedient or lacking in faith.

So what was to be the church's new attitude toward the medical profession? "The Bible simply does not speak in a *condemning* way about physicians in general,[12] my dad wrote, adding that Luke, the author of the third Gospel and the Book of Acts, was referred to approvingly as "the beloved physician." He summed up his new understanding like-this:

Brethren, let us realize that seeking medical attention and having faith in God need NOT be OPPOSITES!

God has nowhere in His Word commanded Christians to avoid doctors, to avoid checkups, to avoid medicines, inoculations or any surgical operation. God can and does supernaturally intervene to heal. Yet He does not ask us to avoid taking such care of ourselves as we have knowledge and facilities available.[13]

My dad announced that the healing booklet had to be temporarily withdrawn until edits and revisions reflecting this new understanding Jesus Christ had given to His Church could be made.[14]

That promised revision came the next year when *The Plain Truth about Healing* was rewritten by my dad and Bernie Schnippert. The booklet made it clear that it was OK to go to doctors. Visiting a physician wasn't a sign of lack of faith in God.

The vast majority of our members were happy with the church's new understanding. But a few emphatically were not. Even then there were rumblings of unrest. Some members were unhappy about the *way* the new understanding had been presented. Because we wanted the booklet to be appropriate and useful for a general readership (and not directed only to our members), in describing the church's former teaching on divine healing we had used phrases such as, "Some have taught..." or "Some have believed..." A few people approached us and said, "What do you mean, 'some have taught'? *You* guys taught us this stuff!" They viewed such language as a cop-out.

Others were upset for another reason. They wondered, *Is this booklet intended to correct a misunderstanding in doctrine? Or has it been issued as a slap at the authority of Mr. Armstrong?* Even some who believed that Mr. Armstrong had made an error on this particular teaching didn't like the new booklet. They didn't object to the thrust of the new teaching; they simply were uneasy that the church would officially declare Mr. Armstrong to be wrong on *anything*. They did not want anyone to open the door on the notion that Herbert Armstrong could be really wrong about something. And now that door was fully ajar.

FURTHER EARLY CHANGES

The next doctrinal changes came on the heels of the first one. Two changes were announced in February 1988.

First, we said that it was no sin to wear makeup. That might sound petty to many readers, but it was a big deal for us. Remember two of the headlines I quoted in the last chapter? "How subtly Satan used MAKEUP to start the Church off the track" and "OUR LIGHT IS SHINING—and not the cosmetics on our faces." Mr. Armstrong had taught, clearly and forcefully, that wearing makeup was a sin that had led God's church into serious error:

> God's Church, the now imminent Bride of Christ, is not going to rise to meet the returning Christ in the air with painted faces and plucked and repainted eyebrows!

How cleverly, without our suspecting it, did Satan influence leading ministers to derail the Church in many ways!...

The Church RULED AGAINST THE USE OF MAKEUP based primarily on specific "do" and "don't" scriptures, rather than the application of the PRINCIPLE of God's Law....

Jesus Christ through me has been GETTING US ALL BACK ON THE TRACK, ready for His return to earth as the KING OF KINGS, and Lord of Lords. The Church, as HIS BRIDE to be spiritually MARRIED to Him, is to rise to meet Him in the air as He descends. Women of the Church, do you think Jesus Christ will say to me, "SEND A PROCLAMATION TO ALL WOMEN IN THE CHURCH TO PREPARE FOR MY COMING. TELL THEM TO GO TO THEIR DRESSING TABLES, PLUCK OUT THEIR EYEBROWS, PAINT IN NEW ONES HIGHER ON THEIR FOREHEADS, AND USE COSMETICS TO MAKE UP THEIR FACES TO MEET ME IN THE AIR"?

No, dear people, I don't think He will have me make such a proclamation. But rather: Wash the dirt off your faces! CLEAN UP your faces!

Now JESUS CHRIST, through His chosen apostle, is going to RULE on this question once and for all!...

My mother and grandmothers did not wear makeup—nor did your great-grandmothers of the same era. How did it get into our mid-and-latter 20th century society? FROM PROSTITUTES!...

Women do not use makeup to PLEASE GOD today—for I can tell you ON HIS AUTHORITY it is NOT pleasing to HIM![15]

Now, most women in our church never wore makeup in the first place, so this verbal barrage didn't much affect them. But some of the women in our church did wear makeup, at least at work. They wouldn't put it on when they came to church, but away from services they hoped to get away with it without being caught. Inevitably, however, a pastor would hear of a member's use of makeup and then the inevitable questions would begin. In 1988, we rethought this prohibition and declared it to be unbiblical. God had no opinion, one way or another, about makeup—unless it took precedence over the pursuit of godliness. As the apostle Peter wrote, "Your beauty should not come from outward adornment, such as braided hair and the wearing of gold jewelry and fine clothes. Instead, it should be that of your inner self, the unfading beauty of a gentle and quiet spirit, which is of great worth in God's sight" (1 Peter 3:3–4). Focusing on the outward simply misses the point; God is concerned about the heart.

Second, 1988 was also the year we pursued accreditation for Ambassador College. This decision upset some of our more conservative members. "Why are you seeking the approval of the world?" they demanded. "God's college doesn't need Satan's approval. God has accredited us, and that should be good enough." Yet we pushed ahead.

With each doctrinal reform we made in those early years, the dissatisfaction and resentment of some of our members mounted. They were sure that we had some kind of hidden agenda or master plan for the complete reshaping of the church. Of course, we never had any such scheme; we simply were responding to the increasing numbers of questions posed by our members after the death of Mr. Armstrong. When the door to doctrinal change was cracked open by our new understanding on divine healing, we should have known that further (and more significant) changes were inevitable. Still, we never expected what was about to happen.

That is, we never expected that the main beam holding together our theological ship would crack and splinter. Yet it did—sooner and louder than any of us had ever imagined.

CHAPTER NINE

THE CENTRAL PLANK CRACKS

B ritish or Anglo-Isrealism is a doctrine of little interest to most Evangelicals. Some with a seminary or Bible college background might remember it as an esoteric doctrine associated with sects and cults, but for those of us in the WCG is was the central plank of our theology. We believed that we were a faithful remnant of the people of God. We believed that we were the true Israel. We observed the Sabbath and the feasts for a very good reason. We were biological descendants of Abraham. We were not Gentiles. This doctrine formed the basis for how we lived each day and for our view of the world and its future in prophecy.

In 1989 and 1990 we took a survey of all our North American pastors, asking them what they thought of British-Israelism, a doctrine that helped shape our church far more than most people realize. Only a small percentage responded. The responses we received fell into three categories:

1. A handful of ministers thought this doctrine was revealed to Mr. Armstrong and should never be questioned.

2. At the other extreme, several said they were aware of serious problems with the idea of the United States being Manasseh, the United Kingdom being Ephraim, and Western Europe being the Ten Lost Tribes of Israel. They knew there were weighty challenges to this idea from both secular history and Scripture.

3. In between was a group who said, "You know, I don't even worry about this."

We found those responses revealing. The doctrine of British-Israelism had been crucial in the thought of Herbert W. Armstrong since he founded the church back in 1933. Yet a number of our pastors either were uneasy with the theory or simply ignored it. How could this be?

WHAT IS ANGLO-ISRAELISM?

Before we begin to understand the place of Anglo-Israelism in the history of our church, we should probably review what the theory teaches. Herbert Armstrong considered it the key to unlocking biblical prophecy and allowed it to shape much of his teaching and preaching.

In a booklet called *Which Day Is the Christian Sabbath?* Mr. Armstrong outlined his fundamental teaching on the subject:

The peoples of the United States, the British Commonwealth nations, and the nations of Northwestern Europe are, in fact, the peoples of the Ten Tribes of the House of Israel. The Jewish people are the House of Judah.[1]

The people of ten-tribed Israel migrated northwest after Babylon overthrew Assyria. They continued their journey into Western Europe, the Scandinavian peninsula, and the British Isles.[2]

After several generations, the tribe of Joseph divided into the *two* tribes of Ephraim and Manasseh which today are the British and American people.

The tribe of Reuben settled in the country that is France today....

The reader, if he has not already carefully read it, should write immediately for our free booklet, *The United States and Britain in Prophecy.* It explains the dumbfounding, astonishing truth that the people of the United States, the British, the peoples of Northwestern

Europe, are, in actual fact, those very "Lost" Ten Tribes of the nation of Israel—and not by birth Gentiles at all![3]

If you have not read much about this dubious theory before now, no doubt you are wondering how such an odd idea could gain such influence over a church. That's what I hope to show in this chapter. (And by the way, don't bother writing for a copy of *The United States and Britain in Prophecy.* You won't get it from us. And therein lies a story.)

WHY CALL IT THE CENTRAL PLANK?

I've called this chapter about why our church discontinued the teaching of British-Israelism "The Central Plank Cracks." Why do I call this theory the central plank? It affected nearly everything we did. Its influence was both pervasive and powerful.

One of the strongest reasons Mr. Armstrong taught Sabbath-keeping so forcefully was that he regarded it as *the* sign that the United States was one of the ten lost tribes of Israel. As long as Americans worshiped on Sunday rather than on the Sabbath, they would forget their true heritage as Israelites—and would be in grave danger of divine judgment.

If Americans lost the Sabbath, they wouldn't know who they were; they would lose the knowledge that they were really Israel. Once they lost the Sabbath, they wouldn't have the physical sign that they were the physical people of God. Herbert Armstrong insisted that this was why America was in such a spiritual decline. Our whole commission was to tell people to start keeping the Sabbath; then they would recover their identity and then they would be ready for the Lord's imminent Second Coming.

Without British-Israelism, much of the reason for a passionate proclamation of the Sabbath is taken away. As one of our study papers said a couple of years ago: "In Mr. Armstrong's eyes, this doctrine directly affected the preaching of the gospel. It gave it power, at a time in world history that the gospel needed more power. Jesus was about to return!"[4]

The version of the gospel Mr. Armstrong preached was that the kingdom of God was not present—it was coming as a future reality—and those who believed and obeyed were going to be rulers and priests in the kingdom. That message overshadowed the essence of the gospel, the life and death and resurrection and ascension of Christ. Mr. Armstrong did not deny those truths; he simply de-emphasized them. He would say things like, "Yes, that happened, and that's what the Protestants are always weeping about. But the message is not about the messenger; this message about the coming kingdom is the message Christ came to deliver. The gospel is this future to which we look forward. That's the *real* gospel. So don't be fooled. Our calling is to preach this gospel to these Israelitish countries first, only then to the Gentiles."

He claimed British-Israelism held the key to unlocking biblical prophecy—it made clear who "the beast" was going to be, who the "ten nations" of Daniel 2 and Revelation 13 were, that Russia was not going to attack the U.S. so no one should worry about that. In Mr. Armstrong's view, Hal Lindsey and other evangelicals writing about prophecy had only part of the truth about prophecy. In Mr. Armstrong's system, the identity of the ten lost tribes was bound up with the proclamation of the gospel.

A few years ago when we realized this theory was unbiblical and actually served to cloud the real gospel, we stopped preaching and teaching it. Thus the central plank cracked. Yet none of us foresaw the effect this would have on our theology as a whole. To a large degree, most of us did not realize (any better than a few of our members still do) how central Anglo-Israelism was to our entire system. When this plank finally cracked, it created a snap heard 'round our theological world.

How did it become our central plank? I think that's an important element of our story.

A BRIEF HISTORY OF ANGLO-ISRAELISM

No one is certain who first originated Anglo-Israelism. Some believe the theory first appeared in 1649 with the publication of John Sadler's *Rights to the Kingdom,* in which Sadler speculated that the English descended from Israel's "lost" ten tribes. Others think a Canadian named Richard Brothers first formulated the theory. Around 1800 Brothers started calling himself a prophet sent by God to warn London of its impending doom. He singled out Parliament for God's special wrath, identifying it as the beast of Revelation to which God gave the number 666. Brothers said it had been revealed to him that the English people were really Israelites. He was imprisoned for a time and died insane in 1824.

While we don't know for certain who originated the theory, we do know that John Wilson had success in popularizing the idea. In 1840 he published *Our Israelitish Origin* to great public demand. Several editions were produced, in both England and America.[5]

Several writers and theorists took over from there. Anglo-Israel supporters got a boost for their theory in World War I when Britain captured Jerusalem from Turkish control. They claimed that Ephraim (the British Empire) had liberated the Holy City in order to give it to their "brothers," the Jews. And it all happened in fulfillment of biblical prophecy, they said.[6]

In 1917 a classic book on the topic was released, J. H. Allen's *Judah's Sceptre and Joseph's Birthright.* Allen's work would soon influence the thought of a few leaders in the Church of God (Seventh Day)—and along with them, Herbert W. Armstrong.

Before he had ever entertained the idea of starting his own church, Mr. Armstrong had become fascinated with Anglo-Israelism...as well as with some other highly esoteric doctrines:

> Through the years, bizarre beliefs have sometimes become attached to Anglo-Israelism. Among the oddest has been pyramidology. Pyramidologists claim that if one correctly interprets the measurements of the inner tunnels of the Great Pyramid of Giza one can know the future. Therefore, they believe that the Great Pyramid was inspired by God to help biblical prophecy.[7]

Mr. Armstrong began to read whatever literature he could find on both Anglo-Israelism and pyramidology. In 1927 he wrote to the Rev. Lincoln

McConnell, pastor of the First Baptist Church of St. Petersburg, Florida, an author on both subjects. Rev. McConnell wrote back:

> The most recent book on The Great Pyramid and a much easier one to read if you want this, is by "Discipulus," and can be had of the same people.... Its special value lies in the fact that it connects Pyramid truth with "British"-Israel truth in a fine way.... I must say that if you really want to KNOW your Bible you will have to get the books on "Anglo-Israel".... You will never know the real truth the BOOK is teaching without this key. This sounds radical perhaps, but you will see when you study it that it's simple truth.[8]

By 1927, Mr. Armstrong was starting to forge some lasting links between Anglo-Israelism and Bible prophecy. And the connections would continue to increase.

MR. ARMSTRONG'S INTEREST IN ANGLO-ISRAELISM

From the beginning, prophecy had played an important role in the life of Herbert Armstrong. It was prophecy that led to his conversion. He said he "realized that the place to start was to prove whether God exists and whether the Holy Bible is His revelation." Ultimately it was his investigation of Bible prophecy that led him to believe in the divine inspiration of the Bible.[9]

Yet when Mr. Armstrong began observing the Sabbath in the 1920s, he didn't do so because he was absolutely convinced it was mandated by God's law. His early writings show he thought the Protestants had a good argument that the law was nailed to the cross (in the terminology of Colossians 2:14). In a letter, Herbert Armstrong asked a Church of God (Seventh Day) leader by the name of A. N. Dugger to help him understand the Sabbath. But Herbert Armstrong started keeping the Sabbath "just in case" it was what God wanted. When he began this practice, he was still attending the Hinson Memorial Baptist Church in Portland, Oregon, as well as fellowshiping with an isolated Church of God (Seventh Day) in the area.

It took several steps for Mr. Armstrong to identify the Sabbath as the "key sign" of God's true church. One of the major steps was his acceptance of Anglo-Israelism. Herbert became convinced that even if the Gentiles did not keep the Sabbath, those who are Israelites should, for God's law demanded it. So if America and the British commonwealth were actually Israel and not Gentiles, then they ought to observe the Sabbath. So Anglo-Israelism and the Sabbath became interrelated, and he began to believe that keeping the Sabbath was a law, not something to do "just in case."

In the late 1920s Mr. Armstrong wrote a test manuscript to quiz the Church of God (Seventh Day) about whether they would accept his ideas. In that paper he presented the Sabbath and Anglo-Israelism as interrelated. The church ultimately rejected his views partly because it had no interest in Anglo-Israelism; it wanted only to promote the Sabbath in the context of what was called the "Third Angel's message."

This teaching was based on a misunderstanding of Revelation 14:6–13. Verses 9–11 of that passage read:

A third angel followed them and said in a loud voice: "If anyone worships the beast and his image and receives his mark on the forehead or on the hand, he, too, will drink of the wine of God's fury, which has been poured full strength into the cup of his wrath. He will be tormented with burning sulfur in the presence of the holy angels and of the Lamb. And the smoke of their torment rises for ever and ever. There is no rest day or night for those who worship the beast and his image, or for anyone who receives the mark of his name."

Early Sabbatarian interpreters declared that the first angel's message in this passage described the proclamation of the gospel in the apostolic age. The second angel's message referred to the Protestant Reformation. The third angel sounded his message as a final warning to the world before the return of Christ. It was especially associated with observance of the Sabbath; some interpreters stated (as some still do) that "the mark of the beast" should be connected with Sunday-keepers who refused to worship on the Sabbath.

Mr. Armstrong took in all this discussion and soon came to believe that God had revealed to him—and only to him—Anglo-Israelism's connection to the Third Angel's Message. By 1929 he believed that God had commissioned him to broadcast this message worldwide.[10] As he wrote, "I was made to see clearly that I have been given a commission to get this warning message out with the loud shout to the world."[11]

By this early date he already saw himself as God's prophet, warning the "Israelites" to prepare for the coming of the Lord. Everything he did thereafter sprang from this belief. Occasionally in his later ministry he would downplay the Anglo-Israelite message, but it continued to pop up all through the years, even in *Mystery of the Ages,* the book he considered his crowning achievement. He was the special messenger called to deliver this end-time warning message to Israel. The message involved the Sabbath, the true gospel, dietary laws, and the holy days. And everything revolved around Anglo-Israelism.

CONNECTING ANGLO-ISRAELISM WITH THE SABBATH

While discussions about the Sabbath and prophecy and Anglo-Israelism were raging in many quarters by the late 1920s, it was Herbert Armstrong who connected the Sabbath with Anglo-Israelism in a unique way:

> The union of Anglo-Israelism with Sabbatarianism later became an important part of Mr. Armstrong's preaching on these subjects. The union he created between these two doctrines explains much of his future work.[12]
>
> In his letter [to A. N. Dugger] Mr. Armstrong presented Anglo-Israelism with a new twist, a twist he hoped would make his book more attractive to Dugger. He claimed that Anglo-Israelism, as he presented it, shed new light on a longstanding Church of God doctrine, the Third Angel's Message. Dugger replied that he would welcome any new infor-

mation Herbert Armstrong could provide on that subject.[13]

Later Mr. Armstrong would come to renounce the doctrine of the Third Angel's Message, but in 1928 he united it with Anglo-Israelism.

To understand why the union, realize that Herbert Armstrong took Anglo-Israelism to its logical conclusion. Previous Anglo-Israelites emphasized God's blessings to Israel. Nobody said anything about the curses.

Herbert Armstrong noticed the curses. He realized that to be consistent, an Anglo-Israelite needed to preach them as well. In Ezekiel, God foretold Israel's defeat and enslavement.

Herbert Armstrong failed to see that Ezekiel was written to Israel in anticipation of Jerusalem's fall in 587 B.C. Beginning from an Anglo-Israelite world view, he saw Ezekiel's references to the House of Israel not as evidence of an Israelite presence in Judah, but as proof that Ezekiel was written to the lost tribes. Ezekiel was, he believed, not for the Jews but for Israel. Therefore, even though Ezekiel clearly spoke of the siege of Jerusalem and the destruction of its temple, Herbert Armstrong concluded that Ezekiel's message had nothing to do with those historic events. He insisted on an Anglo-Israelite interpretation. From this faulty premise he reasoned that God intended Ezekiel's book to be a warning to end-time Israel.

Since Mr. Armstrong believed that the Anglo-Saxons were the remnant of the House of Israel, he believed the message of Ezekiel was a warning for the United States and British Commonwealth.

Herbert Armstrong noticed something else as well. He noticed what he thought were the reasons for the curses. Listed prominently among those reasons was Sabbath-breaking (Ezekiel 20 and 22).

It was then a simple step for Mr. Armstrong to merge Anglo-Israelism with the Sabbatarianism of the Third Angel's Message.[14]

In 1930 Herbert Armstrong wrote: "Unless we know our identity as Israel, we cannot understand the mighty personal warning which the Almighty has published in every English Bible to every individual Israelite.... Just as surely as it was given to God's holy prophets to foretell 2,500 years ago that in the year 1917 a.d. the Army and Air forces of the British throne should take Jerusalem...so he has revealed thru those same prophets what is yet to take place before all things are fulfilled.... These things could never be understood except thru a knowledge of Israel's twentieth-century identity. For instance, the book of Ezekiel is addressed primarily to the United States and Great Britain, and to those of our present generation. In it are recorded events destined to take place within the NEXT SEVEN OR EIGHT YEARS."[15]

Since he had concluded that Ezekiel was written to modern America and not to ancient Israel, Mr. Armstrong then tried to show why America should keep the Sabbath. He transformed God's judgment on ancient Israel for breaking the covenant into an indictment against America for flouting the Ten Commandments.

Yet he saw one major theological hurdle standing in the way of this understanding. Why didn't a great man like Paul, the apostle to the Gentiles, explicitly teach his converts to observe the seventh day? And why were the eyes of such "great men of God as Luther, Calvin, Wesley, Moody, Finney, Cartwright, et al." blinded to this truth? And why didn't "the Holy Spirit lead these men into this truth, when they unquestionably were men filled with the Holy Spirit?"—especially since the Sabbath was "the final test of obedience"? The answer, Mr. Armstrong said, had to do with Israel:

Israel was blinded in part, until the end of the times of the Gentiles (1917–1936)...and in the case of those individuals who repented, and returned to the true God, and accepted salvation, God winked at this blindness....

That is why Dwight L. Moody was blinded to the Sabbath truth!

That is why Luther, Calvin, Wesley, and all these great latter-day men of God were blinded to this truth!

Israel was blinded to it until the fullness of the Times of the Gentiles

HERBERT ARMSTRONG IN 1915 AT AGE 23.

HERBERT WITH MOTHER, EVA WRIGHT ARMSTRONG.

ARMSTRONG'S WIFE, LOMA, WITH DAUGHTER BEVERLY.

ARMSTRONG IN CHICAGO IN 1919 WITH
DAUGHTER BEVERLY, THE FIRST OF FOUR CHILDREN.

THE SALEM, OREGON STORE WHERE ARMSTRONG DELIVERED HIS FIRST SERMON IN THE SUMMER OF 1928.

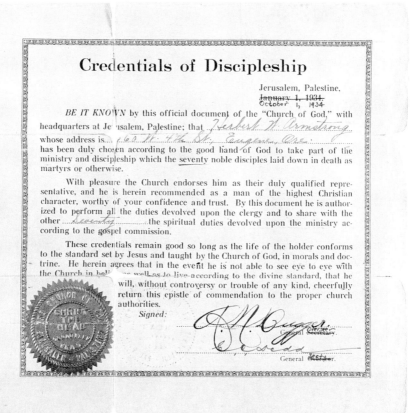

MINISTERIAL CERTIFICATE ISSUED IN 1934 TO HERBERT ARMSTRONG BY CHURCH OF GOD, SEVENTH DAY LEADERS A.N. DUGGER AND C. O. DODD.

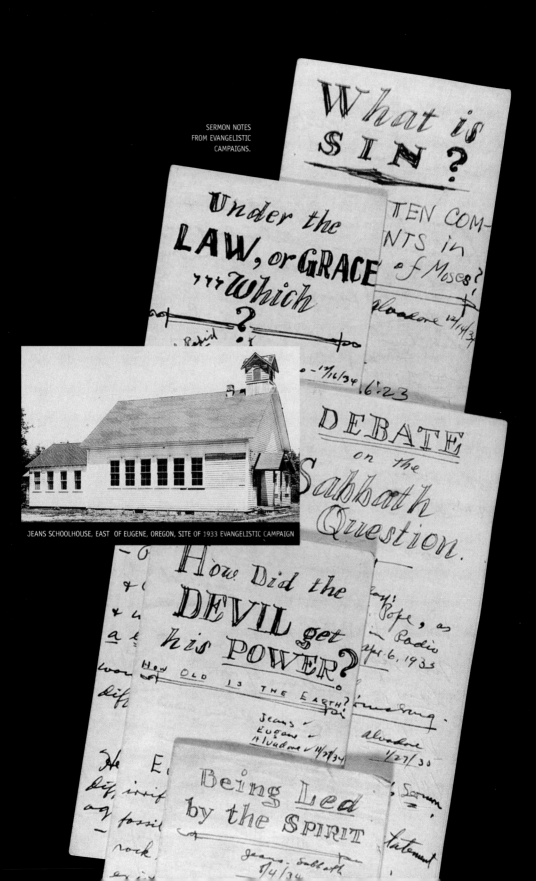

SERMON NOTES FROM EVANGELISTIC CAMPAIGNS.

What is SIN?

Under the LAW, or GRACE ??? Which ?

DEBATE on the Sabbath Question.

How Did the DEVIL get his POWER?

Being Led by the SPIRIT

JEANS SCHOOLHOUSE, EAST OF EUGENE, OREGON, SITE OF 1933 EVANGELISTIC CAMPAIGN

The PLAIN TRUTH

VOL. I NO. I — *Thy Word is Truth* — **February, 1934**

Is a World Dictator About to Appear?

WE Live today in the most strenuous, anxious, momentous hours of earth's history.

Today we stand on the very threshold of colossal events that will stagger the mind of mortal man. Just now it is like the lull before a great and devastating storm. Everyone senses it !

The Lust for World Power

Ever since the Pharaohs in Egypt---on down thru ancient Syria, Babylon, Persia, Greece, Rome---on to Napolian, and the Kaiser---there has been a lust for power to rule the world.

Today at least three major world powers seek to rule the world.

Soviet Russia admits the theory of Communism cannot be perfected until all opposition is wiped out and the whole world is under its sway.

The amazing Tanaka Memorial of 1927, recently discovered and exposed, outlines a most astounding program of Japanese expansion involving the defeat in war of the United States, and Russia, and of the whole world. This program raises Japanese imperialism to the height of insane megalomania. Japan's policies and actions of the past two years supply irresistible proof of preparation to carry out the aims of this document. It is commonly known to

WILL It be Mussolini, Stalin, or Roosevelt?

Everybody senses that something is WRONG with the world . . . that some mighty event is about to occur.

What is it? Bible prophecy tells ! Here is a solemn warning . . . and it is the plain truth !

that Mussolini's whole aim is to restore the ancient Roman Empire in all its former splendor, power, and glory---and Rome ruled the world !

Today Prime Minister MacDonald of Great Britain

HERBERT AND LOMA ARMSTRONG IN THE BROADCAST STUDIO IN THE LATE 1940'S, WITH ELDEST SON RICHARD AT THE CONTROLS.

ARMSTRONG EMERGING
FROM THE CHURCH'S JET
WHICH HE USED FOR
WORLD TRAVEL, MEETING
WITH POLITICAL LEADERS
IN THE 1970'S AND '80'S.

ARMSTRONG CELEBRATES THE 50TH ANNIVERSARY EDITION
OF *THE PLAIN TRUTH* (1984). AT ITS PEAK, THE MAGAZINE'S
UNPAID CIRCULATION EXCEEDED 8 MILLION COPIES.

IN HIS LATER YEARS ARMSTRONG PRESENTS A MESSAGE LIVE FROM
PASADENA, VIDEO TAPED FOR CONGREGATIONS AROUND THE WORLD.

AMBASSADOR AUDITORIUM, PASADENA,
CALIFORNIA. COMPLETED IN 1974,
THE IMPOSING EDIFICE WAS THE SITE OF
CONCERTS FEATURING TOP CLASSICAL
AND JAZZ PERFORMERS FOR 20 YEARS.
IN 1997 THE AUDITORIUM STILL HOUSES
CHURCH SERVICES FOR THE WORLDWIDE
CHURCH OF GOD'S LOCAL CONGREGATION.

JOSEPH W. TKACH, SR., SUCCESSOR OF HERBERT ARMSTRONG AS PASTOR GENERAL OF THE CHURCH, AS A CHILD WITH HIS PARENTS AND SISTERS. FROM LEFT: VASIL TKACH, DAUGHTERS VERA, ANNE AND MARY; FRONT ROW FROM LEFT: JOSEPH, SR., SISTER LILLIAN AND MOTHER MARY.

HERBERT ARMSTRONG AND JOSEPH TKACH, SR. CHAT IN THE CHICAGO AIRPORT IN THE LATE 1950'S.

FORMAL PORTRAIT OF JOSEPH TKACH, SR.

THE SENIOR TKACH PREACHING IN THE LATE 1980'S, AFTER HIS SUCCESSION TO PASTOR GENERAL.

A YOUNG JOSEPH TKACH, JR., WITH HIS PARENTS,
JOSEPH, SR, AND ELAINE.

JOSEPH TKACH AT HIS
FATHER'S FUNERAL WITH
HANK HANEGRAAFF.

TAMMY AND JOSEPH TKACH.

(Rom. 11:25), because God did not desire the House of Israel to be identified or known by the world until then.[16]

Since Mr. Armstrong believed that "the Times of the Gentiles" ended in
1917, it follows that he would come to believe it was in that year that the Sabbath became "a final test of obedience." And since Luther, Calvin, Moody, Finney,
and the rest all lived before that time, naturally they would have been "blinded"
to this Sabbath truth.

In our day, however, there would be no such excuses. God could no longer
"wink" at such a major transgression of His law. Keeping the Sabbath was paramount, as Mr. Armstrong insisted in his booklet *Which Day Is the Christian Sabbath?:*

> God commanded His people to keep His Sabbath as a *sign*. It is a sign
> between God's people and God—"...a sign between me and you," the
> Commandment says. It is a badge or token of IDENTITY. It advertises,
> or announces, or proclaims certain identifying knowledge. But what
> knowledge? God answers: "...that ye may know that I am the Lord that
> doth sanctify you."
>
> Note those words carefully! It is the sign that identifies to them who
> is their God! It is the sign by which we may know that He is the Lord!
> It identifies *God!*[17]
>
> The Sabbath also was given as a sign which identifies who are the
> people of God and who are not.[18]
>
> How significant! The Sabbath command is the only one of the ten
> which is a sign identifying who are the real and true Christians today! *It
> is a real TEST command!*[19]

The reason why the House of Israel came to be known as the "Lost Ten
Tribes," according to Mr. Armstrong, was that they had lost their national identifying sign, the Sabbath. So he concluded, "Yes, the Sabbath, God's day—the

true Lord's day—is, after all, the day for our people doubly—first, because it was made for all people, even Gentile-born people who are now, spiritually, through conversion, Christ's; secondly, because racially, even by flesh birth, it is God's day which He gave our own forefathers, and commanded to keep holy forever!"[20]

CONSEQUENCES OF THE DOCTRINE

As I said, our acceptance of Anglo-Israelism affected practically everything we did. It helped shape what we preached, to whom we preached, how we spent our money, where we spent our time, how we related to various ethnic groups.

I think there were a number of people who didn't think of themselves as racists, who really tried to operate on a racially neutral perspective. Nevertheless, in the back of their minds, there existed this Anglo-Israelite doctrine that silently worked to foster racial prejudice. As much as our members might have tried to treat everyone equally and with respect—a few people tried actively to fight against racism in our midst—they faced an uphill battle as long as this doctrine held sway among us. Anglo-Israelism had a profound effect on how we wrote about social issues in the sixties. It explains why we viewed the Civil Rights movement so negatively—we viewed it through an Anglo-Israelite perspective.

I agree wholeheartedly with the conclusion reached a couple of years ago in a study paper done by one of our ministers, Ralph Orr, on Anglo-Israelism:

> It saddens us when Christians erroneously justify their racist attitudes through misuse and misunderstanding of the Bible. While one might expect that those new in the faith might harbor racial prejudice, as God's Spirit leads them, they should come to see how poisonous such thinking is. They should then seek God's help in conquering such attitudes. Unfortunately, some found the Anglo-Israel belief in *The United States and Britain in Prophecy* as excuse enough not to repent of racism....
>
> In the Church, non-Anglo-Saxons sometimes found fellow Christians looking down on them simply because they were not "Israelites."

To these people, being German, African-American, Hispanic, Asian, Ukrainian, Italian, Polish (or a member of any other ethnic group) was to be inferior. Perhaps as a form of psychological self-defense, a few of Eastern or Southern European descent would speculate that, perhaps due to Israel's wanderings, they were Israelite, not Gentile. It somehow seemed inferior to be 100 percent Gentile. Obviously, such views do not belong among God's people.[21]

REJECTING THE THEORY

Within two years of Mr. Armstrong's death, several church leaders began discussing Anglo-Israelism with my dad. The more we studied, the more its "biblical" and "historical" foundations began to crumble. And for good reason.

When you start carefully reading Anglo-Israelite literature, you begin to notice how it generally depends on folklore, legends, quasi-historical genealogies, and dubious etymologies. None of these sources proves an Israelite origin for the peoples of northwestern Europe. Rarely, if ever, are the disciplines of archeology, sociology, anthropology, linguistics, or historiography applied to Anglo-Israelism. Anglo-Israelism can operate only outside the sciences. And its handling of the biblical data is no better. To make many of its conclusions plausible, it must ignore large portions of Scripture which would immediately puncture it with holes the size of football fields.

Such an unscientific and unbiblical approach must be taken because anything else would pop Anglo-Israelism's balloon. We discovered that those who apply sound hermeneutics, scientific disciplines, and the principles of accepted historiography to this subject eventually dismiss the theory. That is certainly what happened with us.

In June 1988 my father withdrew *The United States and Britain in Prophecy* from circulation.[22] Soon thereafter all mention of Anglo-Israelism disappeared from the church's publications. We stopped sending out *The Book of Revelation Unveiled at Last.* We stopped sending out *Who Is the Beast,* which essentially identifies Sunday-keeping (as opposed to Sabbath-keeping) as the mark of the beast.

In July 1995, the church announced in the *Pastor General's Report* that Anglo-Israelism lacked any credible evidence and that the church would no longer teach it. This was followed by a study paper sent to the ministry giving detailed reasons why this was so.

We had come to believe that Anglo-Israelism had distracted us from giving our full attention to our truly God-given commission—the preaching of the good news of salvation through Jesus Christ and the duty to make disciples of Christ of all nations.

In 1995 we wrote the following in our study paper titled *The United States and Britain in Prophecy:*

> In the past the Worldwide Church of God has taught that *The United States and Britain in Prophecy* explained an important key that unlocked biblical prophecy—the identification of the Anglo-Saxon peoples as the leading representatives of the lost tribes of Israel. We reasoned that God commissioned his end-time Church to warn those peoples of his coming wrath. *The United States and Britain in Prophecy* was one of our principal means of fulfilling that perceived commission.
>
> The foundation of our faith and preaching is not *The United States and Britain in Prophecy.* The foundation of our faith is Jesus Christ, the One who has commissioned us, the One in whom we have faith and the One we seek to imitate.
>
> Of course we have always preached that Jesus is our Savior. Nevertheless, for many of us, it has not been our central and foremost message. Some have erroneously thought that *The United States and Britain in Prophecy* was the primary message God wanted us to preach to the world. This is evident from those who have expressed concern that failure to distribute that book meant we were not doing God's work. As we have already seen, such a view is biblically unsound.[23]

We do not insist that our members give up their personal belief in Anglo-Israelism if they wish to maintain such a conviction, but our church no longer endorses or teaches the theory.

WHAT NEXT?

Whether or not we or our members or ministers perceived Anglo-Israelism as essential, once it was dethroned, a major support for many of our distinctive doctrines quickly fell away. What would fill the void? Our answer would get to the heart of the gospel—to Jesus Christ Himself. He would fill the void, for that is His rightful place. Yet when we began speaking more and more about Jesus, a question kept coming up. It's a question that deserves a chapter all its own.

CHAPTER TEN

WHAT'S ALL THIS "JESUS STUFF"?

How could we get our people to take their focus off British-Israelism as a central plank of their faith and get them instead to see that Christ is *the* central plank in a Christian's belief system? That was the major challenge facing us a few years ago.

To help achieve this we decided to address the topic at several regional conferences to be attended by all our pastors and lay elders. In one of my presentations I said, "We're not going to put out this British-Israelism teaching anymore. You're free to believe it if you so desire, but it's an unprovable theory. If you want to hold on to it, that's okay; you're entitled. But consider this: The knowledge of the identity of the lost ten tribes does not forgive your sins; it has no redemptive quality. It does not improve your marriage. It does not help your parenting. It does not help you relate better to other people. In fact, it tends to do the opposite—it tends to breed racism. So in the final scheme of things, where does knowledge of these lost tribes really fit? When you compare it to knowledge of your Savior, how vital is it? Isn't Jesus the One you need to know?"

Many people reacted to my comments by saying, "Yes, that's right. Jesus ought to be our focus." But a significant number of disgruntled listeners said, "Wait a minute! What's all this Protestant doctrine you're teaching? What's all this love-love fluff? What's all this Jesus stuff? I came out of that. The church I went to for fifteen years before I came here, that's what it preached every week. It was always Jesus this, love that. You never learned anything else. It was boring!"

Wherever I went I heard: "What's all this Jesus stuff?" I heard that question half a dozen times a day, every day, for the better part of two years.

AN INFAMOUS SERMON

And I was far from the only one to field this query. One of our pastors, Ralph Orr, gave a sermon in Seattle in which he addressed the issue of preaching the gospel versus preaching Anglo-Israelism. "I naively assumed that most of the other pastors had addressed the subject," Ralph told me. "In fact, only one of them had. So I talked about how every dollar spent on warning about Europe attacking the U.S. is one less dollar spent on the gospel.

"I was unprepared for their reaction. People didn't want to hear this. They wanted to hear that the coming kingdom of God, the millennium, was the gospel. 'What's all this Jesus stuff?' they asked. Unquestionably, there was an element of the church that opposed hearing regularly about Jesus."

Part of that "element" still remains. Recently a man who has been attending one of our splinter groups, the Global Church of God, visited one of our services in Pasadena. One of our senior ministers, Ron Kelly, spoke about the seven miracles that Jesus performed as described in the Gospel of John without quoting the text directly. At the end of the service our Global visitor, obviously perturbed, approached me and demanded, "Did you think that was a good sermon? Do you approve of that sermon? He didn't read one verse!" The man ignored the fact that the whole sermon was about seven specific miracles Jesus had performed and that Ron *had* quoted several verses in his message. But I don't think that's what rankled him the most. I think what irritated him was hearing a whole sermon about Jesus. This man represents many of our former members (and perhaps a few current ones) who did not want to hear much at all about Jesus. Our new emphasis on Jesus as the centerpiece of our faith did not and does not sit well with these folks.

WHO WANTS TO BE A PROTESTANT?

Outside observers no doubt are curious about how our church had come to the place where it downplayed the person and ministry of Jesus. The fact is, our people had been programmed not to talk much about Jesus. While we thought it was great to wax eloquent about Abraham and Isaac and Jacob and David and Solomon and Elijah and Elisha and the rest of the heroes of the Old Testament—and even wonderful to delve into the life stories of lesser-known characters such as Zerubbabel and Ezra and Melchizedek—Jesus was not a frequent topic of conversation. We loved the Old Testament and spent a great deal of our time there. This Old Covenant bias permeated our entire organization. If several years ago you had listened to our radio broadcast, it's much more likely that you would have thought you were hearing the sermons of a Jeremiah than those of a Paul. We focused on the Old Testament God and minimized the new emphases developed and highlighted in the New Testament.

Even when we did cross over into the New Testament, we tended to focus on such giants of the faith as Paul and Peter and James (we really liked James). But Jesus? We didn't spend too much time on Him. That was something the Protestants did; we thought we'd just leave it to them. That was all the namby-pamby, sloppy stuff anyway.

When at last we did get around to talking about Jesus, we had a characteristic way of referring to Him. Almost always we would use His "full" name, Jesus Christ. To us, it was almost like saying "Mr. Christ." To refer to Him using only the name "Jesus" would be to sound like a Protestant—a weak and detestable thing. To use the name "Jesus" by itself was to speak of the weak Jesus, the baby Jesus, the effeminate Jesus, the syrupy, sloppy, pathetic Jesus. And we wanted none of that.

In an odd way, we had an almost negative predisposition toward Jesus. It was nothing we had planned, nothing official. But since we had distanced ourselves from Protestants and since they spoke so much of Jesus, we didn't. Who wanted to sound like a Protestant? Who wanted to talk like a member of one of the harlot daughters of Babylon?

What we believed at the time about Jesus Christ was well summarized by Mr. Armstrong:

Jesus came 1) to overcome Satan and QUALIFY to establish the KING-DOM OF GOD; 2) to call and teach His future apostles; 3) to proclaim the GOOD NEWS of the coming Kingdom of God; 4) to pay the penalty of the sins of the world by His death on the cross with His shed blood, thus reconciling *those called* to contact with God the Father; 5) to be res-urrected from the dead after three days and three nights in the tomb, making the resurrection to IMMORTAL LIFE possible for those who are God's; 6) to ascend to the throne of God in heaven, there, as the HIGH PRIEST of the Church and ITS LIVING HEAD, to direct the Church and intercede for it with God. And 7) having received the Kingdom from God, to COME AGAIN as the KING of kings and LORD of lords, in supreme almighty POWER and GLORY, to set up and rule THE KING-DOM OF GOD![1]

Rather than speak much about Jesus, we talked mainly about God. He was the Father, and He was in charge. And of course, since we didn't believe in the Trinity, we were never really quite sure what to do with Jesus. Throughout most of our years as a church, we struggled with theological inconsistencies about Him. We never developed a consistent doctrine of Christ, a biblically based Christology. We did say He was divine. But we said He was divine only before and after the incarnation, as though God is not God all the time. So on the one hand we said things that denied the deity of Jesus, but on the other hand we said things that affirmed Jesus' deity. We believed Christ had come to tell us to obey the law and to prepare for the coming kingdom, which only law keepers would inherit.

When we discussed Jesus, we would normally focus on the biblical refer-ences where Jesus talked about the coming kingdom. We insisted that this mes-sage was the main message, far and away the most important message. Sure, Jesus came to die on the cross, rise again, and make it possible for believers to live forever; but this was secondary to His main objective: to restore the kingdom of God in the future.

It is significant that in Mr. Armstrong's list above, the idea that Jesus came "to pay the penalty of the sins of the world by His death on the cross with His shed blood, thus reconciling *those called* to contact with God the Father" is only number four on the list of seven. On the other hand, three items in his list focus on the coming kingdom. Notice that he both begins and ends his list with references to the kingdom, a kingdom that is to come in the future, at the time of the Second Coming. That was not accidental. In our theology, Jesus Christ was primarily a messenger, a proclaimer of the coming kingdom of God. As Herbert Armstrong put it:

> Jesus Christ was sent into this world as a messenger bearing the most vital and important message ever sent from God to mankind. This was foretold by the prophet Malachi. His message was the greatest NEWS ANNOUNCEMENT ever to fall on human ears. It should have rocked this world and shaken it to its foundations. The word *Gospel* means *good NEWS!* It was news of an earthshaking *future* event.
>
> Jesus' Gospel—the message He brought to humanity from God—was the good NEWS of the Kingdom of God—the soon-coming WORLD GOVERNMENT of the almighty GOD to rule all nations and bring us PEACE at last! Also, His stupendous announcement included the fact that humans, on repentance and faith, could become actual begotten children of God, could be BORN AGAIN—born of God, entering that Kingdom when set up.[2]

Of course, it is true that Jesus *did* proclaim the coming kingdom of God, forcefully and often. The first reference is found in Matthew 4:17: "From that time on [after the temptation in the desert] Jesus began to preach, 'Repent, for the kingdom of heaven is near.'" Just a few verses later Matthew tells us, "Jesus went throughout Galilee, teaching in their synagogues, preaching the good news of the kingdom…" (Matthew 4:23). In the first Gospel alone, God's kingdom is mentioned no fewer than forty-nine times. One of the last references to the kingdom in Matthew's Gospel shows the serious nature of preaching the kingdom: "And this gospel of the kingdom will be preached in the whole world as a testimony to all nations, and then the end will come" (Matthew 24:14).

So there is no doubt that the kingdom of God is essential to Jesus' teaching and message. But was the kingdom only a *future* reality? Was Jesus merely a messenger, a newscaster proclaiming primarily *future* events? If so, what did He mean when He said, "I am the resurrection and the life. He who believes in me will live, even though he dies; and whoever lives and believes in me will never die" (John 11:25–26)? If so, why does all of the preaching in the Book of Acts center not on the kingdom but on the death and resurrection of Christ? If so, what did the apostle Paul mean when he wrote to the Corinthians: "When I came to you, brothers, I did not come with eloquence or superior wisdom as I proclaimed to you the testimony about God. For I resolved to know nothing while I was with you except Jesus Christ and him crucified" (1 Corinthians 2:1–2)?

Eventually we came to see that we had all but ignored the many times when Christ preached His identity and His saving work. We did not ponder deeply enough the vast implications in Luke 4 when Jesus went to the synagogue in Nazareth, opened the scroll of Isaiah to a well-known Messianic text, read it aloud, rolled up the scroll, handed it back to the attendant, sat down, and then said to the crowd, "Today this scripture is fulfilled in your hearing" (Luke 4:21). We did not linger long enough over His words to the Jews, "I tell you the truth, before Abraham was born, I am!" (John 8:58). We did not meditate earnestly enough on passages such as John 5:16–18:

So, because Jesus was doing these things on the Sabbath, the Jews persecuted him. Jesus said to them, "My father is always at his work to this very day, and I, too, am working." For this reason the Jews tried all the harder to kill him; not only was he breaking the Sabbath, but he was even calling God his own Father, making himself equal with God.

In recent years we have returned to these texts and others like them and have been forced to reevaluate the person and message of Jesus Christ. We have found that the message Jesus brought was the message that the "light has shined in the darkness" in the person and saving work of the Son of God. This is the message of the kingdom of God. Jesus rules already in the church He calls His own, and His kingdom will continue to advance until the day He returns to judge the world and bring all things under the dominion of the Father.

THE POSITIVE SIDE

I need to back up for a moment to make sure that no one thinks the WCG ever knowingly minimized Christ. On this issue our church did, at the very least, focus on Christ every spring. At Passover time (historically, we used Old Covenant terminology for even New Covenant revelation—we now refer to this service as the Lord's Supper) every year, our congregations worldwide recited the story of the death and resurrection of Jesus Christ. We recalled the reason for His death. We ate the bread and drank the wine that memorialized His sacrifice on our behalf. In this way, once a year, we were reminded of what Jesus did for us. In the weeks leading up to Passover, some ministers took extra time to preach about the meaning of Jesus' sacrifice. In this way, a reminder was always kept before us of what Jesus accomplished at the cross on our behalf.

And at other times, our church and its leaders held up Jesus in many ways. Mr. Armstrong took the lead here. It was common for him to say things like this:

> To God I said, "YES, SIR!" In utter sincerity, I literally GAVE MYSELF to Jesus Christ. He had bought and paid for me with His life's blood. He OWNED me. I BELONGED TO HIM! I became a YES-MAN to Christ![3]
>
> Brethren, I am Christ's chosen apostle, and I know Satan is a thousand times stronger than I. I have to rely on CHRIST, who is MORE POWERFUL than Satan.[4]

Some people are surprised to learn that Jesus was central to our faith, but He was. It's just that His role as Model Human Teacher and Judge was given far greater emphasis than His role as Redeemer, Savior, and Friend. My friend Ralph Orr recounts his experience:

I came from a mainline denomination where the pastor of the church undermined the Christian faith. I was made a member of that church without even knowing if there was a God. I could see the hypocrisy at the heart of that, of making me a member while I didn't even know if Jesus ever lived, if he was a real person of history or whether he was just a literary creation.

Meanwhile, the Worldwide Church of God, on its radio and television broadcasts and in its written literature, did at least occasionally address the main questions about Jesus: Was he a historical figure? Did he perform miracles? Did he fulfill prophecy? As a teenager I came across this material, read it, and was intrigued. But it was the church's radio broadcast that really hooked me. I specifically remember Garner Ted Armstrong saying that Jesus must have been raised from the dead—how else could you get twelve marine-types to make up such a story, then for decades to suffer all the difficulties the apostles did, and yet not one of them ever confess to lying? That was a convincing argument to me. In addition, some of our church's literature dealing with Isaiah 53 and Psalm 22 and the book of Daniel convinced me that Jesus was the Messiah.

So there were elements in what the church taught that did bring me to Jesus. Of course, it also brought a lot of other stuff along with it. But no one should think that the church failed to bring *anybody* to Jesus. There were people such as myself—and I've met others who said that formerly they were atheists, agnostics, etc.—who came to a living faith in Christ when they heard what the church was teaching. They became convinced that there was a God, that the Bible was his Word, and that

Jesus was their Savior. It's just that they also all took on a whole lot of other excess baggage.

Perhaps some of the members who have stayed with us through the recent changes have been those members for whom Jesus has been more important than some of these other things. A large percentage of our ministers said they didn't bother with Anglo-Israelism. That raises an interesting question: what *did* they bother with? I think some of them bothered with Jesus. That was the focus of many of our members. My wife, for example, never much bothered with Anglo-Israelism; she couldn't understand it, anyway. I believe there were many in our church like her.

I believe Ralph's conclusion is correct. Despite the tangential issues which sometimes took center stage in our church, many of our members focused on their relationship to Christ and were growing in Him long before the past few years when the official doctrinal changes began to reshape the WCG. Our mailbox provides me with evidence to support this belief. While a large number of the letters we have received over the past few years can be characterized as angry and hostile, we always have gotten a few precious letters from members encouraging us to maintain our current course. One longtime member who has been with us for more than twenty years wrote to my father in the months before he died:

Many of the doctrinal changes concerning the new covenant and a magnification of the law of love are inspiring and should create a whole new dimension in the church.... The scriptures have been in the Bible for centuries and God's way of life is not going to pass away.

I'm having some difficulty in understanding why some think these things are new. It's been years since I believed that keeping God's law would gain me any spiritual advantage—I never believed it would gain me salvation. I firmly believe that only Christ's shed blood is what God sees when he looks at me—like the blood splashed on the doorposts for the Israelites when the death angel passed over.

We have twenty-four hours a day—365 days a year—to fill with some kind of activity and keeping the commandments and the Holy Days structures those days for me. Within that framework I can build good deeds of love and caring for my family and others....

Many of us in the church have been living the law of love and sharing and caring for years.[5]

I pray that this dear woman's attitude is even more widespread among us than I have dared to hope. Our elevation of Jesus to His rightful position of majesty and glory is not a new teaching, any more than have been the other doctrinal changes that led up to it. The Bible has proclaimed this message all along. All we have done is to take seriously Mr. Armstrong's instruction to find out what the Bible teaches and then go and follow it. This isn't always easy, but it is always right. We are grateful to God for the increasing light He has shined in our hearts and minds. When we think about where He has already led us, we are profoundly thankful—and we remember that He leads us still.

NO OVERNIGHT CHANGES

Our change in attitude toward Jesus didn't happen overnight. A series of changes led up to it. In 1989 we stopped circulating booklets that taught what we had come to believe was a flawed understanding of divine healing.

In 1991 came a bigger change. We began to teach that our destiny as humans is *not* to become divine, as we formerly insisted. We had taught our people that we were to become "very God" or even "God as God is God." We used to teach that although we were going to be equal to God, we would never be identical to God, since He is eternal. We had a beginning, of course, so God would always stay a step ahead of us. We came to this conclusion through a collection of misunderstood biblical words and misinterpreted verses of Scripture.

Until recent years, we insisted that God was literally reproducing Himself in us. We took great pride in the fact that we were the only church to understand and preach these phrases as God intended them. We reasoned that if God has sons, he must be reproducing Himself just as a snake has a snake, a cow has a cow, and humans have humans. So if God has children, they must be Gods.

Finally we realized the Bible doesn't say this. When we started to grasp the nature of God, we discovered that we're not going to be Gods, but rather we have already become the adopted children of God.

A number of our members were very troubled when they heard the church was no longer teaching they would become Gods in the God family. They asked, "Then what *are* we going to become?" When you have been taught for years that you would become God, then you hear you're *not* going to become God, what's left? There was a tremendous amount of discomfort among our people prompted by their belief that we had taken away the very purpose for human existence.

For quite some time people asked me questions about it. I would say, "It's true that we will not become God, but there *is* the resurrection and immortality. Isn't that sufficient? We will receive glorified bodies, just like that of Jesus after His resurrection. They will never grow old or wear out. Isn't that enough?" It was tough for many of our members to accept that; it just didn't seem good enough. For many of those who have left us, this probably still remains the case. They continue to equate the teaching of their future Godhood with the good news; for them, anything else is a denial of the gospel.

(The Global Church of God still teaches that their members become Gods. The United Church of God equivocates. On the one hand they concur with the historic teaching of Herbert W. Armstrong. "Mr. Armstrong's 18-point list of restored truth, while not a doctrinal statement in itself, stands confirmed in its essentials by the board.[6] On the other hand, they downplay Mr. Armstrong's historic emphasis by usually speaking of our eternal inheritance as becoming "children of God.")

As we dug deeper into Scripture, we continued to make changes and corrections. In 1991 we also said it's inaccurate to teach that someone is only conceived (and not born again) when he or she accepts the gospel. Until that time we had taught that believers were born again only at the resurrection. But that is an error. We had misunderstood Jesus' teaching in John 3 and had somehow missed what Peter wrote in 1 Peter 1:23: "For you *have been* born again, not of perishable seed, but of imperishable, through the living and enduring word of God." Today we teach that true believers are born again the moment they believe. It's easy to prove this by using any good lexicon; you can look it up for yourself.

Soon after this change we found it necessary to discuss how the church should use the term "apostle." For years (but not always) Mr. Armstrong had called himself "Christ's apostle," and when we started announcing these changes, people kept coming to us and saying, "Well, Mr. Armstrong was an apostle. How can you say that so many of the things he taught are wrong? He was an apostle equivalent to the twelve and these things were revealed to him. The things he taught are equivalent to canon in Scripture. You can't just change them!"

We replied that while it was proper to use the term *apostle* as an ecclesiastical title to denote the highest rank in our church, it was wrong to make Mr. Armstrong an apostle equivalent to the original twelve. That troubled some people.

Every one of these changes heaped another straw on the camel's back. None of us knew when it might break, but that was beside the point. One of the major themes of Mr. Armstrong's ministry had been that we should follow the lead of the Scriptures no matter what. He would often say, "Don't believe me, believe the Bible." That's exactly what we were committed to doing.

In 1993 we were led to see (and thus began to teach) that Jesus is *eternally* God's Son. In the past we denied this. As Mr. Armstrong had written: "Jesus Christ did not become the Son of God until about 4 B.C. when born in human flesh from the Virgin Mary. Prior to that He had ALWAYS existed, even as had God."[7] This did not square with Scripture. How could the One who is described as "the same yesterday and today and forever" (Hebrews 13:8) change so radically in something as fundamental as his relationship to the Father?

In 1993, following logically on the heels of that doctrinal change, we also started to teach the Trinity. Of course, that change was not met enthusiastically.

For decades our church had taught that the Trinity was a pagan doctrine. My good friend Mike Feazell, who grew up in our fellowship, has joked that he used to think "false-pagan-Trinity-doctrine" was one word! We argued that the historic professions of faith, such as the Nicene Creed, limited God to three persons and that in fact God was comprised (or would be comprised) of a "God family" with the Father at its head, Jesus Christ immediately behind Him, and all of us following Him as glorified, born-again God beings. We had also denied the personality and personhood of the Holy Spirit:

> If the Holy Spirit is not a Person—a Ghost—then what does the Bible reveal about the Holy Spirit?
>
> The Holy Spirit is the Spirit (not Ghost) that emanates out from both God and Christ everywhere in the universe. Through His Holy Spirit, God projects Himself, in Spirit, everywhere in the universe—yet both God and Christ have form and shape, even as man.
>
> The Holy Spirit is many things. It is the VERY LIFE of the immortal God, which, entering in a human, begets him with GOD-life.
>
> It is the POWER of God, by which, when Christ "spake" it was done. It is the POWER by which God stretched out the heavens—created the vast endless universe.
>
> The Holy Spirit, entering into man as God's gift, opens the mind to UNDERSTANDING of spiritual knowledge, unknown to the human mind otherwise. It is the LOVE of God "...shed abroad in our hearts..." (Romans 5:5). It is the FAITH of Christ, which may be given to God's begotten children through the Holy Spirit. It is the POWER of God, begotten within humans, enabling us to overcome Satan and sin.[8]

As we studied the Bible and honestly tried to come to grips with its teaching, we saw this was wrong. The Bible insists there is but one God but makes it equally clear that the Father, Son, and Holy Spirit are God. That means the Trinity must be true.

The more we studied the Scriptures, the more we saw that we had misunderstood. The ancient creeds were right after all; the Trinity was fully biblical. We offically admitted we were Trinitarians by 1993. This proclamation was the last straw for some people. They started to leave our church in greater numbers.

CHAPTER ELEVEN

How Could We Have Believed These Things?

Sometime ago I was talking on the air with Hank Hanegraaff during a live *Bible Answer Man* radio program. In discussing the many changes that have shaken the WCG during the past several years, I used the term "cognitive dissonance" to describe what often went on in our heads in decades past. In many instances we championed two flatly contradictory doctrines at the same time.

After the program Hank and I discussed this idea at more length. Hank thought the idea of cognitive dissonance could provide the foundation for a great book. Such a book, he said, would try to show how people can equally embrace two opposing ideas, concepts that cannot both be true at the same time. I agreed and gave him several quick examples of this phenomenon in our own church.

"You know, Joe" he said after I was done, "this dynamic is present in the kingdom of the cults."

"I imagine it is," I replied, with more than a little conviction.

I still marvel at how we could have believed one thing while noting that reality showed something vastly different. How could we simultaneously have held two radically conflicting ideas in our minds? Why did we not see the obvious contradictions?

WE'RE ALL AT RISK

Before anybody starts shaking his head too much at our checkered history, let me hasten to say that *everyone* suffers from some measure of cognitive dissonance. Psychologist and author Dennis Coon has this to say about the issue:

> Cognitions are thoughts. Dissonance means clashing. The influential theory of cognitive dissonance (Festinger, 1957) states that contradicting or clashing thoughts cause discomfort. We have a need for *consistency* in our thoughts and our perceptions. If individuals can be made to act in ways that are inconsistent with their attitudes, they may change their thoughts to bring them into agreement with their actions.
>
> For example, smokers are told on every pack that cigarettes may endanger their lives. They light up and smoke. How do they resolve the tension between this information and their actions? They could quit smoking, but it may be easier to convince themselves that smoking is not really so dangerous. To do this, they will seek examples of people who have lived long lives as heavy smokers, and will associate with other smokers who support this attitude. They will also avoid information concerning the link between smoking and cancer.
>
> Cognitive dissonance theory also suggests that people tend to reject new information that contradicts ideas they already hold, in a sort of "don't bother me with the facts, my mind is made up" strategy.[1]

I wonder if Coon read our mail? The degree of cognitive dissonance in a religious sect or cult is staggering. It's mind-boggling. Yet for decades we ignored it, skipped right over it without pausing to breathe. I guess that's what intrigues me so much.

As I write this, I'm forty-five years old. From the age of five I grew up in this church—and for most of my life I cruised along with dozens of major contradictions elbowing each other in my head, yet without ever suspecting their constant warfare. I see this as a disease that continues to afflict so many today. Until someone sits down with these folks and starts examining and critiquing their clashing ideas, they will likely remain just as oblivious to them as I was for so many years.

Consider with me just five areas in which massive cognitive dissonance went unnoticed and unchallenged in our church for so long.

WHOM SHOULD WE WORSHIP?

The first example is a classic. Until recent years, it was common for us not to worship Jesus as Lord. Rather, we worshiped God the Father. Certainly we would pray in Jesus' name or in praying we might say, "We're praying to the Father with Jesus at His right hand." But worshiping Jesus was something we simply did not practice. We thought it was wrong to pray to Christ, although it was OK to mention his name at the end of the prayer.

To us, Christ was virtually a dead Savior. We referred to the Lord's Supper as Passover, following the Old Covenant terminology. Talking and fellowshiping at any time during this annual service was strongly discouraged. It seemed to be solely a funeral service.

We taught that our Lord did indeed suffer and die on the cross to pay for our sins, but we spent almost no time celebrating His resurrection, even though that fact was at the heart of our faith. We held that Christ's primary role was as a messenger to announce the coming kingdom. Of course this was part of our teaching that, in essence, denied the full deity of Jesus. Yes, He saved us from our sins through His death on the cross, but that was not the main event; the main event was the coming kingdom of God. While Christ was our means of access to the Father, He himself received little or no worship.

And yet...

Even as we insisted we were to worship God, not Christ, we also taught that if we followed Christ's earthly example—that is, if we did the same things He did during His ministry—then one day we would ourselves be worshiped! We taught that if Christ lived in us and if we emulated His example and thereby achieved sufficient success, then in the future, when Christ returned and we were changed into spiritual beings, *we* would be worshiped by all those who were not yet changed.

Talk about cognitive dissonance!

We were *not* to worship Christ, yet if we lived as He did while on earth, we *would* be worshiped. How is it possible that we did not see the contradiction? I marvel at how long I failed to see the lack of logic behind accepting both these teachings. The error is so clear to me now, but for more than twenty-five years the contradiction never dented my consciousness. It makes no sense, yet for decades the impossibility of both teachings being true escaped our notice.

GOD IS IMMUTABLE...OR; IS HE?

The immutability of God is one point of doctrine our church has always taught. That is, we have always insisted that God the Father is perfect and does not change. We often quoted verses where this truth is found, including one passage where the word *immutable* itself is used:

> God, willing more abundantly to shew unto the heirs of promise the immutability of his counsel, confirmed it by an oath: That by two immutable things, in which it was impossible for God to lie, we might have a strong consolation, who have fled for refuge to lay hold upon the hope set before us. (Hebrews 6:17–18, KJV)

> For I am the LORD, I change not; therefore ye sons of Jacob are not consumed. (Malachi 3:6, KJV)

> Every good and perfect gift is from above, coming down from the Father of the heavenly lights, who does not change like shifting shadows. (James 1:17)

On this point, at least, we agreed with the vast majority of the orthodox Christian church. God is separate from us, distinct in nature, and immutable. He does not change.

And yet...

We also taught that *we* were going to become God and be God in the same way *He* is God. As Herbert Armstrong wrote in 1981:

In man God is reproducing Himself. We shall be as much God as God Himself is God. It will be a Family of God, a God Family. God the Father will always be at the head of that whole Family. Jesus Christ will always be next in that Family. The rest of us at the resurrection, at the time of the Second Coming of Christ, will be the Bride marrying Him. The husband, Christ, will rule over the wife, the Church, and Christ will be ruling next to God.[2]

Of course, the historic Christian church did not agree at all with us here! While we taught that we would become God, even this paragraph shows that we also insisted we would never be completely identical to God. God was forever going to be a couple of steps ahead of us; in His learning cycle He would always grow and learn ahead of where we were. Therefore He would "always be at the head of that whole Family."

It's not hard to see where the cognitive dissonance lies in these two opposite positions, is it? On the one hand, we said God doesn't change, He's immutable; on the other hand, we taught that He's growing and learning and forever a step ahead of us. In a very real sense, this is the most liberal process theology there is.

How could you get any more contradictory? Yet we didn't see any difficulty at all. It's not that we saw the contradiction and tried to defend it; we simply didn't see the problem. We could confidently proclaim that God is perfect and immutable and would even quote the verse, "I am the LORD, I change not"— then turn around and say, "God is growing and changing, and one day we will be God."

Of course, it's got to be one or the other. It can't be both.

Tragically, virtually all the major groups that have broken away from the Worldwide Church of God continue this historic, heretical teaching that human destiny is to become God. This error was at the heart of Herbert W. Armstrong's teachings.

THE BEST CHURCH AND THE BEST MARRIAGES

We used to proclaim in our services and brag in our sermons that the Worldwide Church of God was the only true church. Just look at us: We had the right name, the "Church of God" (see Acts 20:28; 1 Corinthians 1:2; 10:32; 11:16, 22; 15:9; 2 Corinthians 1:1). We had the most honest people, godly men and women filled with integrity. Not only was the Worldwide Church of God the one and only true church, but it was also the *best* church as evidenced by its superior marriages.

Some of our ministers would make this boast to their congregations, and our people strongly believed the claim. They were convinced that our church fellowship had the best marriages of any church in the world. How could you tell that God was in our midst? Because the quality of our marriages so far outshined those in any other denomination.

And yet...

The truth is, we didn't have the best marriages. We had just as much divorce and remarriage as any other church. To this day, most of our members and former members are oblivious to the fact that we averaged about three hundred divorces a year. As a denomination, we had just as many troubled marriages and people needing marriage counseling as any other religious group in America. The survey of our ministers that we do every year consistently told us that the number one problem in our fellowship was conflict and difficulty in marriage.

That, friends, is called cognitive dissonance.

On the one hand, we said we were the best church because, among other things, we had the best marriages in the world. But on the other hand, the number one problem in our church, year after year, was our marriages. How could we say we had the best marriages? We could say it because we wanted it to be true; cognitive dissonance clouded our eyes.

Besides the marriage claim, we also used to trumpet our church's superiority by pointing to our members' level of commitment.

And yet…

We never had the extraordinary level of commitment from our members that we see today in the missionary programs of other denominations. I saw a statistic the other day that claimed more than one hundred thousand people lost their lives for the sake of Christ in this past year alone. More missionaries are being killed today than at any time in history. Yet that never happened with us. Our missionary work consisted largely of exporting our American church culture.

As a fellowship, we remained largely unaware of Christian missionaries, their work and sacrifices, until these past few years.

FAILED PROPHECIES

One of the more peculiar dynamics of WCG history is that our flagship publication, *The Plain Truth* magazine, formerly contained vast amounts of prophetic speculation. Our intention was to help explain world events in light of biblical prophecy. We were so locked into our prophetic schemes that we tended to see prophetic fulfillment in almost every news item. One of the most common predictions was that very far in the future (yet here and now), the Nazis were rising up again to take over Europe. We would often point out how the news fit into our predictions of a united Europe and the coming of the Antichrist.

Consider just a few such headlines and excerpts from articles Herbert Armstrong wrote in the late seventies and early eighties:

- In a page one article headlined, "Where Are We Now in the Panorama of Prophesied World Events?" Mr. Armstrong started out, "The death of Pope Paul VI may trigger a drastic change in world events. This change could plunge the world into the most terrifying crisis ever experienced by man."[3] Later in the article he wrote, "The meeting of the Catholic College of Cardinals in the Sistine Chapel at the Vatican may well prove to be a WORLD-SHAKING EVENT—the most important world event since World War II!"[4]

- When the former Soviet Union invaded Afghanistan in 1980, Mr. Armstrong wrote, "In the past two weeks, this world has entered into a 'whole new ball game.' The intervention of the Soviet Union in Afghanistan changes the whole world picture."[5] A few pages later he asked, "Can WE discern the signs of the times? END-TIME EVENTS are going to happen FAST from here on! The 80s well might see the END of this present world; WAKE UP!"[6]

- A few months later Mr. Armstrong wrote, "Signs are now fast appearing that our Work of the GREAT COMMISSION may be much more near completed than we have realized."[7] And in a related article in the same publication he ventured his prediction that "God's great work through His Church (Philadelphia era) may be FINISHED in a matter of months."[8]

- On June 30, 1980, Mr. Armstrong wrote, "This present election travesty may well be the very LAST political election for the presidency of the United States, with little incompetent men vying for the coveted prize."[9]

- On March 6, 1981, Mr. Armstrong said that "conditions in the world fulfilling biblical prophecies are now fast accelerating, indicating that we are indeed in the very last of the last days"[10] and predicted that "terrible, frightful things are going to happen in the next few years that are going to take the lives of probably two thirds or more of all the people now living on the face of the earth."[11]

As these predictions of impending doom indicate, we were convinced the world was about to end and that God was poised to set up His kingdom at any moment. We firmly believed this and boldly proclaimed our beliefs for everyone to hear.

And yet…

While we did manage a few correct calls, we also made more than *one hundred* prophetic predictions that failed. For one, we said that Europe was going to unite and take the American and British people into subjection and slavery. We predicted this would happen by the early 1970s—and of course, it didn't.

The sad fact is that for fifty years we predicted the end of the world would come in just four to seven short years. When those four to seven years passed into history without our predictions coming true, we'd say that the world would end in *another* four to seven short years. This pattern repeated itself many times. Only when decades came and went and still the world hadn't blown itself to pieces did we finally begin to notice the cognitive dissonance. We started to realize we couldn't keep saying such nightmarish events would happen in four to seven years when, in fact, *fifty* years had come and gone without any of our apocalyptic prophecies being fulfilled.

I think our experience has much in common with that of a group led by a certain Mrs. Keech, a woman mentioned in Coon's psychology textbook as a notable example of cognitive dissonance:

> Mrs. Keech was receiving messages from superior beings on a planet called Clarion. On their journeys to Earth, they had detected a fault in the earth's crust that would submerge the North American continent in a natural disaster of unimaginable proportions. The date of this event was to be December 21. However, Mrs. Keech and her band of followers, who called themselves the Seekers, had no fear of the impending disaster. Their plans were to assemble on December 20 when they expected to be met at midnight by a flying saucer and taken to safety in outer space.
>
> The night of December 20 arrived, and the Seekers assembled at Mrs. Keech's house. Many had given up jobs and possessions in preparation for their departure. Expectations were high and commitment was total, but as the night wore on, midnight passed and the world continued to exist. It

was a bitter and embarrassing disappointment to all concerned.

Question: Did the group break up then?

The amazing twist to this story, and the aspect that intrigued social psychologists, was that the Seekers became more convinced than ever before that they and Mrs. Keech had been right. At about 5 A.M. Mrs. Keech announced that she had received a message explaining that the Seekers had saved the world. Before the night of December 20, the group had been uninterested in convincing other people that the world was coming to an end. Now they called newspapers, magazines, and radios to explain what had happened to convince others of their accomplishment.

How do we explain this strange turn in the behavior of Mrs. Keech's doomsday group? The answer seems to lie in the concept of *cognitive dissonance*.[12]

We, too, did our share of "explaining" why certain predictions failed to come to pass. And just as in the experience of those who followed Mrs. Keech, our prophetic failures did little to convince us that something was wrong.

These days, what can we say about a unified Europe and the approach of Armageddon? For one, we notice that trends in Europe continue to move both *toward* unity and *away* from it. It is impossible to say, from looking at such data alone, that the end is near. We have learned that not every major political development is a fulfillment of biblical prophecy; not every catastrophe is a harbinger of imminent judgment. I suppose that if the floods and windstorms that swept over California in early 1997 had occurred thirty years before, they most certainly would have made the cover of *The Plain Truth* as evidence that the world was going to end in a few years. In reality, of course, the California floods and windstorms were no more devastating than many others in the history of this nation.

So the question keeps rising to the surface of my mind: How is it that for more than fifty years we couldn't see what should have been so plain? It was right in front of our eyes. One or two failed prophecies might well be ignored—but more than a hundred of them? At long last, the cognitive dissonance between failed prophetic speculations and historical reality became too much even for us to bear. We gave up on frequent predictions—yet somehow we still clung to the flawed framework that made them possible.

And Herbert W. Armstrong wasn't the only one caught up in prediction addiction. Consider some of these historic predictions from the pen of Roderick C. Meredith, who now leads one of our splinter groups, the Global Church of God. The predictions below were written while he was a minister in the World-wide Church of God:

> 1957—"After 1965, we are destined to run into increasing trouble with the Gentile nations. America and Britain will begin to suffer from trade embargoes imposed by the brown and oriental races.... We will begin to experience the pangs of starvation and the scarcity of goods!"[13]
>
> 1963—"You might as well wake up and FACE FACTS! The world you live in won't be here 15 years from now!"[14]
>
> 1965—"Frankly, literally dozens of prophesied events indicate that this final revival of the Roman Empire in Europe—and its bestial PERSE-CUTION of multitudes of Bible-believing Christians—will take place within the next seven to ten years of YOUR LIFE."[15]

The Global Church of God is merely one of a number of splinter groups that continue to dust off failed predictions and reinsert new dates, over and over again. Just a few days ago I was shown the following quotation from Garner Ted Armstrong, who along with his father, has given one failed prediction after another. In the first issue of a newsletter Ted wrote, "The 'strongman' of Europe is Germany, just as I have been saying and writing for the past forty-two years, and just as my father before me predicted even as World War II was coming to a close."[16]

What Ted Armstrong fails to point out is that we all have been living for over two decades in an America that, according to his predictions, shouldn't exist. The predictions he speaks of—the ones he gave in writing, on the air, and in sermons for forty-two years—were laced with specific times and dates when America would be destroyed by Germany.

It is with profound sadness that we in the Worldwide Church of God see such delusion, such cognitive dissonance. We know that there, but for the grace of God, go we. And our prayers are that God will touch the hearts of those still gripped by such cognitive dissonance, those who are suffering from prediction addiction.

THE TRUE CHURCH: DEAD OR ALIVE?

In a classic article titled "Seven Proofs of the True Church" from the late 1970s, Herbert Armstrong offered the following version of church history:

> By about A.D. 59 the Gospel Jesus Christ proclaimed had been suppressed (Galatians 1:6–7). A counterfeit gospel had replaced it. From about A.D. 70 there ensued "the lost century." All historic record of the true Church of God had been systematically destroyed during that hundred years—the curtain had been rung down on Church activities, and when the curtain of recorded history lifted an entirely *different* church appeared, calling itself Christian. Extreme persecution of powerful forces had driven the true Church of God underground.
>
> The church by the fourth century was more like the Babylonian mystery religion, having appropriated the name "Christianity." (Revelation 17:5)[17]

In other publications and at other times Mr. Armstrong preferred the date of a.d. 53 as the year of the church's demise. Yet in general his teaching on this point remained fairly static: The true church was persecuted and destroyed about a.d. 53 and remained *in absentia* until God restored it to the world through Mr. Armstrong, beginning in the twentieth century. As Mr. Armstrong wrote, "Could anything sound more unbelievable? To say the true Gospel of Jesus Christ was not proclaimed during 19 whole centuries—from the middle of the first century until the middle of the 20th—may sound preposterous! Incredible! But TRUE!... The Gospel Jesus brought from God, proclaimed and taught His apostles was the prophetic message of the coming KINGDOM OF GOD. Yet THAT GOSPEL was SUPPRESSED about or just past the middle of the first century and was not again proclaimed to the world until 1953—19 centuries later—and THEN by the present living generation of that same ONE and ONLY true original Church of God, established by Jesus Christ a.d. 31!"[18]

We believed this wholeheartedly and taught it forcefully.

And yet...

Herbert W. Armstrong also taught that the true church continued to exist through seven eras of time, each one represented symbolically by the seven churches of Asia Minor listed in Revelation 2 and 3. The WCG embodied the faithful Philadelphia-era church, the next-to-last era in world history. Only the Laodicea-era church—the apostate church—remained.

Do you see the problem with this? How could we say that the true gospel wasn't preached since A.D. 53, yet maintain that the church survived (at least in an underground form) for nineteen hundred years? It makes no sense.

And beyond that obvious contradiction, it is a fact (one which we never disputed) that much of the New Testament wasn't even written by A.D. 53. If the true gospel had not been preached since A.D. 53, then how did we get the New Testament? Who wrote it? Paul's letters are generally believed to be the first parts of the New Testament to be written. The first one, probably 1 Thessalonians, was penned around A.D. 51; the last one, 2 Timothy, was not written until A.D. 66–67, when the apostle was imprisoned and then executed by the Roman emperor Nero. Now if the church truly ceased to exist after A.D. 53, then what are we to say about the legitimacy of Romans (about A.D. 57), 1 and 2 Corinthians (A.D. 55), and the rest of Paul's letters? And what should we do with all four of the Gospels, the earliest of which (Mark) likely was not written until the late A.D. 60s?

The statement that the true gospel had not been preached to the world since A.D. 53 simply doesn't match history. Even if it were true, how could it be that the church continued to exist through the same period? It's an obvious contradiction, yet no one seemed to notice it. Why not? Probably we viewed the ancient church as a secret, underground society that existed all through this time. The statement that the true gospel wasn't preached for eighteen and a half centuries was really an attack aimed at all other churches. We unwittingly replaced true, authentic, documented church history with a giant conspiracy theory.

I realize this doesn't clear up the contradiction, but that's the thing about cognitive dissonance. Explanations don't have to make sense, they simply have to give security and some peace of mind. Ours did.

IS MODERN MEDICINE OK TO USE?

Earlier in this book I described the last example of cognitive dissonance that I'd like to mention, but I think it bears repeating. On the one hand, we taught that using modern medicine to battle disease and illness demonstrated a lack of faith. Calling upon the services of a doctor for anything beyond an accident, setting bones, childcare etc., merely showed that your faith was insufficient and small.

And yet...

Herbert Armstrong, the very one who taught us that using modern medicine showed a lack of faith, used the medical profession, especially in his later years. Mr. Armstrong visited doctors for his heart condition and took several medications to maintain his health.

So what were our members to think? This point was difficult for some people to accept. We hoped that what Mr. Armstrong practiced would lend some balance to what he wrote, but our hopes were not always realized. Sometimes when we pointed to Mr. Armstrong's practice as a corrective to what he wrote, members got angry and perceived our words as "Armstrong-bashing." They could not accept that what he practiced spoke just as loudly as what he preached and wrote. In the case of those members (who in many cases became former members), the cognitive dissonance continues unabated.

THE ONLY ULTIMATE REMEDY

There is no doubt that, to one degree or another, cognitive dissonance afflicts us all. Virtually all Christians say they want to spend more time with their families, yet many of us work ever-increasing hours. As Christians we decry lawlessness in society, yet some believers cheat on their taxes. We claim that we care about the plight of the poor, yet we Americans give less than three percent of our incomes to charity. That's cognitive dissonance!

Cognitive dissonance also permits us to believe two contradictory ideas at the same time. Frequently you hear of someone who believes God's Word is true yet also believes premarital sex is OK, or that Jesus died for the sins of the whole world yet there are many ways to God. Both can't be true at the same time, yet the same individual can profess belief in each doctrine simultaneously.

While all of us suffer from some measure of cognitive dissonance, my friend Hank Hanegraaff is certainly correct when he asserts that this "disease" reaches massive proportions within sects, cults, and churches with infirmed doctrine. "Massive cognitive dissonance" is surely the right description in our case. For decades we believed doctrines that absolutely contradicted one another, or we adhered to teachings that simply did not match observable, demonstrable fact.

The apostle Paul helps us to understand this phenomenon. In his words, "the god of this age" had blinded our eyes so that we could not "see the light of the gospel of the glory of Christ" (2 Corinthians 4:4). People who are blind cannot see. How do you explain light to someone who lives in perpetual darkness?

Now that by God's grace the veil is being lifted, however, we *do* see His glory—not all of it, but a breathtaking portion of it—and we find the sight stunning beyond words. In an ultimate sense, the only sure way to dispel massive cognitive dissonance is to be so bathed in the true brilliance of the gospel that "the light of the knowledge of the glory of God in the face of Christ" shines in our hearts (see 2 Corinthians 2:6). We are finding that in that kind of light, darkness cannot continue to exist. We bank on that promise, because we've had too much of the night.

ADVISORY

To all current or former members of the Worldwide Church of God:

PLEASE READ THIS FIRST!

This chapter is not written to attack or belittle Herbert Armstrong in any way. I will not dare to judge the quality of his spiritual relationship with God—that's not for me or anyone else to attempt. I believe that God loved him, that he loved God, and that his security rests in Christ alone. This chapter represents my personal attempt to come to grips with the central place Mr. Armstrong holds in the history and shaping of our church.

CHAPTER TWELVE

THE ENIGMA OF HERBERT W. ARMSTRONG

As I write these words, I'm working in the office once occupied by Herbert W. Armstrong. I'm sitting at the desk Mr. Armstrong used, and I'm looking out the windows that once served as his eye on the world below. Everywhere I turn my head there are reminders of his strong leadership and pervasive influence. As I gaze on his portrait and glimpse mementos from his world travels that are scattered throughout our Pasadena headquarters, I feel compelled to try to make sense of what has happened in the Worldwide Church of God since his death in January 1986. So I sit in Mr. Armstrong's former office, trying to look back and understand the man who led our church for so many years.

THE HARDEST CHAPTER TO WRITE

I'll be honest with you: This chapter is the hardest one in the whole book for me to write. There are many reasons why this is so.

First, Mr. Armstrong himself was a very complex man. It's not always easy to understand the motivations that drove him or the influences that helped shape him. He could be both loving and harsh, gracious and antagonistic, humble and proud. He is not an easy man to categorize.

Second, my task in this chapter is difficult because I know my readers come from one of at least two vastly different audiences. One group is made up of people who greatly admire Mr. Armstrong and everything he said. They will be watching closely to see if I attack my former mentor and spiritual leader. The other group is at the other end of the spectrum. Its members want me to denounce Mr. Armstrong, to call him a false prophet who led thousands of people into serious spiritual error.

I am afraid that I will disappoint both groups, for I won't be taking either of these two options. I intend neither to canonize Mr. Armstrong as a sinless saint nor to condemn him as a hateful heretic. My goal is to try to come to some understanding of who he was as a man and as a leader, as well as to see how he laid the foundation for where we stand today in the Worldwide Church of God. It is necessary to be honest about the errors that he taught, yet it is appropriate to show respect to him as the founder of a movement that taught Jesus as being the only name under heaven by which we can be saved.

Regardless of what you may personally think of Herbert W. Armstrong, one fact is incontrovertible: The overriding reason our reforms have developed and taken root is that Mr. Armstrong himself always insisted that those who want to follow God must find out what God's Word really says, then go and do it. As we have followed his instruction in the past few years, we have discovered many things in our church that needed to be changed.

To avoid running ahead of that story, however, I think it would be helpful to jump back to the beginnings of the Worldwide Church of God. The following is by no means an exhaustive history of our founder and the denomination he created, but it should help you understand where our church came from and where we have been.

IN THE BEGINNING

Herbert W. Armstrong was born in 1892 to Quaker parents in Des Moines, Iowa. He would later say that the religious training he received in his formative years taught him a system of beliefs but nothing of vital spirituality as a way of life.

As a young adult Mr. Armstrong worked as an advertising agent and from 1912–1915 wrote advertising copy for *The Merchants Trade Journal*. In 1920 his own advertising business was wiped out in what he called a "flash depression." He moved to Oregon in 1924 and soon saw two more businesses fail. Around this time he began to get more serious about spiritual matters.

In the early years of Mr. Armstrong's ministry, before he was attracted to Anglo-Israelism, Pyramidology, and Adventism, he was strongly influenced by evangelical Christianity. This fact is little known. Most of our members have long thought they were not Protestant—hardly a surprising development since we were taught we had an independent history from "the whore of Babylon and her daughters." On the other side, many books critical of Mr. Armstrong talk only about the cultish sources which allegedly influenced him. Some cultish and aberrant groups did influence him—the Jehovah's Witnesses, or Adventism for example—but these books ignore the significant influence of the evangelical community (see appendix).

This evangelical influence is one of the strongest reasons Mr. Armstrong consistently pointed to the Bible as his final authority for faith and practice, as opposed to church tradition or an outside source. Believe it or not, our "culture" in the church always has been closest to evangelical Protestantism. Where did this influence originate?

In the midtwenties Mr. Armstrong frequently consulted with an evangelical minister and was baptized by the pastor of the Hinson Memorial Baptist Church in Portland, Oregon. Mr. Armstrong once said of this pastor, "The man is the most godly man in all of Portland." There is some reason to suppose that Mr. Armstrong attended the Bible school which was associated with Hinson at that time; this Bible school met at the Portland library at the time Mr. Armstrong was beginning his studies.

We also know Mr. Armstrong used the Scofield Reference Bible, the favorite Bible of dispensational evangelicals during that period. He said the Scofield Bible helped him understand some important doctrines, especially the dispensationalist view of prophecy. Perhaps it was the pastor of Hinson Memorial who introduced him to Scofield's Bible. Whatever the case, Mr. Armstrong later adapted those prophetic views to an Anglo-Israelite model.

Yet even this was not the full extent of the evangelical influence on Herbert Armstrong's teaching. His first wife, Loma, was a Methodist, and the perfectionism often found in Methodism eventually was incorporated into the teachings of our church. In addition, when he was beginning his own evangelistic efforts, Mr. Armstrong said he had read and admired the works of Charles Finney, the great nineteenth-century American evangelist. Finally, the evidence indicates that Mr. Armstrong learned his stance on healing from Pentecostal sources. While he rejected their tongues-speaking, he accepted some form of their doctrine on healing. Our archives show that when some people in Los Angeles wanted prayer for healing, he pointed them to the Pentecostal mission downtown.

Of course, Mr. Armstrong didn't stay long with mainstream evangelicals. By the mid- to late-twenties, he had begun to search elsewhere for spiritual truth. When his wife told him she had come to believe that the Bible taught Christians should worship on the Sabbath, not on Sunday, Mr. Armstrong said he vigorously disagreed and set out to prove her wrong. Yet at the end of several weeks of intense study, he said he was "completely converted, spring of 1927" to the Sabbatarian point of view.[1] Shortly after that, he and his wife began fellowshiping with a Church of God (Seventh Day) group in Salem, Oregon. Mr. Armstrong began preaching to small crowds in 1930.

There is some controversy about whether Mr. Armstrong and his wife ever became members of the Church of God (Seventh Day). Throughout his ministry he loudly insisted he never was a member, that he provided help and encouragement to this group but never joined. Yet several extant documents dispute this. A memo from the Bible Advocate Press (affiliated with the Church of God, Seventh Day) in Denver, Colorado, offers the following history of the time in question:

Mr. Herbert W. Armstrong began his search for "truth" (in earnest) back in the Fall of 1926 after his wife, Loma, had embraced the seventh-day

Sabbath message as the result of the witness of a Church of God woman.

Mr. Armstrong to that time had considered his wife's acceptance of the Sabbath as an indication of "religious fanaticism." So he set out to prove her wrong. In the spring of 1927, Mr. Armstrong accepted his wife's views as correct.

It was about that time that Mr. Armstrong entered into the Church of God fellowship. According to Mr. Armstrong, he felt that the Church of God in Oregon embraced the truth and the testimony of Jesus, but it was a fruitless work. So he has contended that he and Mrs. Armstrong maintained "a detached fellowship."

That "detached fellowship" did not prevent Mr. Armstrong from accepting a ministerial license from the Oregon Conference of the Church of God (Seventh Day). The Oregon Conference was an affiliate of the organization which at that time was headquartered in Stanberry, Missouri. The ministerial document was issued in about 1931. Back in those days state conferences were empowered by the General Conference to grant ministerial licenses, with the General Conference granting credentials. The General Conference was composed of state conferences, each of which was an association of congregations. The state conferences were totally dependent on the General Conference offices for their authority.

(Some folks have inquired of the Armstrongs' membership status. The Church of God *did not ever* issue ministerial documentation to non-members.)

In 1933 the Church of God (Seventh Day) suffered a severe schism, dividing right down the middle. The half that severed (both in members and ministers) established their headquarters in Salem, West Virginia. This new organization was headed by Andrew N. Dugger, who had served as president of the old conference from 1914 to 1928 and as editor of the *Bible Advocate* from 1914 to 1932. The two divisions reunited in 1949, eventually establishing new headquarters in Denver,

Colorado. A small number of dissidents remained separate from the reorganized body, and kept a skeletal work in Salem.

Mr. Armstrong gravitated toward the Salem movement. He had aligned himself with A. N. Dugger, thus following Elder Dugger in that association.

By 1934, Mr. Armstrong had accepted appointment as one of "the seventy," a group of ministers and church leaders who were charged with "the message for the last days."... Mr. Armstrong was granted ministerial credentials at that time.

It was also about this time that Mr. Armstrong began a radio broadcast ministry which he identified as "The Radio Church of God," and which he later contended to be independent of the Salem body's support or endorsement. Interestingly enough, the Salem body was publishing his reports and articles at the time, so apparently they did not share his understanding. He was carrying the highest documentation that the Church bestows.

During the ensuing months and years, Mr. Armstrong began to take an outspoken view on his understanding of British Israelism and the Hebrew feasts. The brethren encouraged him to present to the ministerial body as a whole his views on those subjects, rather than to continue preaching and promoting most forcefully his personal position.

It was at Detroit, Michigan, that Mr. Armstrong's material on the Hebrew festivals was presented. The ministerial body gave full treatment to the positions of Mr. Armstrong and a majority rejected the doctrine as unscriptural. But Mr. Armstrong was most insistent and continued to present his viewpoints in an antagonistic manner.

So, in 1938 the Salem organization revoked Mr. Armstrong's credentials. Official records show the doctrinal dispute to be the reason for the severance.

In a "summary of copies of letters on file at the General Conference offices regarding Mr. Armstrong's affiliation with the Salem movement successive to the

1933 division," the memo calls attention to a form letter which Mr. Armstrong signed which "required each minister's allegiance to 'the Constitution of the Church of God, with world headquarters at Jerusalem, Palestine.'" Attached to that form is the following note: "Will you please record this my acceptance, and have credentials issued to me, according to my ministry in the body? Sincerely, Herbert W. Armstrong, 1142 Hall St., Salem, Oregon." Another letter dated August 15, 1934, states, "I feel that my views and my stand, and what I preach, are in harmony and accord with all these '40 points' [that is, the 40 points of doctrine as outlined in the Constitution of the Church of God (Salem, West Virginia)]."

Mr. Armstrong later wrote that "The parent local church of the present WORLDWIDE CHURCH OF GOD was the Church of God at Eugene, Ore., organized in August, 1933, with 19 members."[2] From that year until 1968, the church enjoyed growth of about 30 percent each year—something Mr. Armstrong often noted with pride. Almost all the growth could be attributed to the church's magazine, *The Plain Truth,* and later to its television program, *The World Tomorrow.* In response to this growth, Ambassador College was founded on October 8, 1947, largely to provide ministerial training for the church's increasing number of pastors and lay elders. What they learned at Ambassador was largely the esoteric doctrine of the church. Here's how Mr. Armstrong outlined what he considered to be the three most critical doctrinal distinctives of his church: "The real TEST COMMANDMENT of God's law is the Sabbath. Another was the truth of U.S. and British true identity as the birthright tribes of the 'lost' 10 tribes, the house of Israel. Another was the annual Holy Days."[3]

On this foundation the church continued to grow quickly. In 1953 Mr. Armstrong began broadcasting in Europe via Radio Luxembourg, thus introducing his message to the rest of the world. Rapid growth continued until the 1970s, when it slowed substantially. Herbert Armstrong's mission seemed to change after the death of his first wife in 1967. He started to delegate much of what he called "The Work" to others, including his son, Garner Ted Armstrong, while he began to travel around the world on the church's G-II (and later a G-III) jet to meet with foreign dignitaries. (One book I read featured a little section that always stuck in my mind. It said, "If you want to make your CEO ineffective, make him a world traveler." Mr. Armstrong did become a world traveler and did become ineffective in the daily operations of the church.)

Eventually several problems came to Mr. Armstrong's attention, and he was forced to take action. His son, Ted, was removed from broadcasting for four months in 1972 for a series of moral and doctrinal failures (the official word was that Ted was "in the bonds of Satan"). That was also the year a major prophecy by Herbert Armstrong failed to be fulfilled: He had erroneously predicted that the Great Tribulation would begin and that the WCG would be miraculously transported to Petra, Jordan, where the church would be physically protected. We generally referred to this event as "fleeing to a place of safety." Some have said this was our version of the rapture.

Our booklet *1975 in Prophecy* predicted the return of Christ in that year; but when it too failed to come true, Mr. Armstrong began to be more careful in his prognostications. He reasserted his control over the teaching and practice of the church and took action against certain leaders who were trying to systematize church doctrine. Ted was officially disfellowshiped in 1978 for his "liberalism" and "modernizing" tendencies. As Herbert Armstrong wrote in February 1979:

> I can tell you how my son, when he was executive vice president, with a small group of liberals at headquarters, tried to bring us into harmony. Some of the ministers did not believe many of the doctrines Christ had put into His Church. A minority (yet perhaps close to a dozen field ministers) had liberal leanings—did not believe the SAME THINGS Christ had put into His Church. So, *behind my back*—unknown to me, while I was in another part of the world carrying Christ's Gospel message into other nations—they produced what they called a Systematic Theology Project, *changing* and *watering down*—making more liberal—many doctrines Christ had put into God's Church.[4]

The Systematic Theology Project (STP) was actually one of the most positive steps the WCG had ever taken. By this time several ministers in Pasadena were engaged in studying and systematically recording church doctrine, under Garner Ted Armstrong's authority. Ted claims he had his father's blessing; Herbert Armstrong later said this was all done behind his back and while he was "out of town."

The STP later became the target of those who were "loyal" to Herbert W. Armstrong. Copies of the STP were trashed and destroyed. Ministers loyal to Herbert Armstrong claimed that the STP was a conspiratorial plot to change "everything" Mr. Armstrong taught.

Of course any examination and detailed study will raise questions. For a brief period of time in the midseventies, we began to liberalize a number of prohibitions regarding dress, use of cosmetics, and several other minor issues. But the charges against the STP were effective, with some ministers claiming that the Systematic Theology Project in fact more accurately stood for Slowly Turning Protestant.

PERSONAL CHANGES

In 1977 the widowed Herbert W. Armstrong married divorcee Ramona Martin. He was eighty-five, she was thirty-nine; they divorced in 1981. In 1979, while Armstrong was living in Tucson, Arizona, the attorney general of the state of California tried to take control of the church, charging that it had violated several statutes. The following year the suit was dropped.

In the years just prior to his death, Mr. Armstrong himself changed some minor doctrines, shaking a few members' belief that he was an infallible teacher of biblical truth. Yet by the time he died in 1986 at the age of ninety-three, Mr. Armstrong left behind a church that attracted 120,000 people to services each week, with an annual worldwide income of about $200 million. *The Plain Truth* circulation was more than eight million, while *The World Tomorrow* television program had risen to become one of the most watched religious programs in America.

POSITIVE CONTRIBUTIONS

When I look back at the long life and career of Herbert W. Armstrong, I am struck by several things. On the one hand, he was passionate about discovering biblical truth and was deeply committed to living by it; on the other hand, many of the doctrines he championed were flawed and unscriptural. He taught that people were not saved by law-keeping but by the grace of God through faith in the death and resurrection of Christ, yet he also taught that God would finally save only those who obeyed Him, including obedience to WCG teachings such as observance of the Saturday Sabbath and the annual holy days. His teaching minimized the sufficiency of the saving work of Christ and emphasized the coming millennial kingdom. He often characterized Christ as little more than a divine messenger.

To this day I am not certain how to relate to the memory of Herbert W. Armstrong. He was my spiritual leader and teacher for almost forty-five years, and it was through his ministry that I came to a saving knowledge of Jesus Christ; yet as I sit in the chair he once occupied, I have come to recognize how far short our church had fallen from biblical norms. He dogmatically taught an inaccurate view of church history which amounted to one gigantic conspiracy theory. There are, however, several lasting and positive legacies Mr. Armstrong bequeathed to us.

1. Respect for the authority of Scripture

From his earliest to his last days, Mr. Armstrong maintained a reverential respect for Scripture. He believed and taught that Holy Scripture was the very Word of God, faithful in all respects and utterly worthy of our loyalty and obedience. As he wrote, "Our teaching and doctrines MUST COME FROM GOD! Through CHRIST!... Jesus Christ is the Word of God in PERSON. The Bible is the same Word of God IN PRINT!"[5]

He would often say that if it could be shown that something he was teaching was unbiblical, he would change his teaching, since the Bible can make no error. It was this strong heritage that created the rails along which our doctrinal train has been running these past few years. Without the deep commitment to the Scriptures which God instilled in us through Mr. Armstrong, we would never have embarked on the journey we have taken. It was this passionate dedication to the truth of the Bible that has emboldened us to make the corrections that Scripture demands.

2. Use of media as a pre-evangelism tool

If you take our former doctrinal aberrance out of the mix, the Worldwide Church of God under Herbert Armstrong led the pack in using electronic and print media to reach unchurched people.

When you hear the history of radio evangelism, you often hear of men such as Charles Fuller but almost never of Herbert W. Armstrong. Yet, an outsider who was not a committed evangelical Christian would ask, "Why are you leaving out one of the top radio and television ministries not only in the United States but the world?" In numbers and impact on his audience, Herbert Armstrong (and his son, Ted) had far greater influence than many other ministries.

Early on, Mr. Armstrong recognized a way to get his message out to an interested audience. The first radio broadcast aired in October 1933, and the regular weekly program, which became *The World Tomorrow* program on radio, began January 7, 1934. He was one of the pioneers; he built one of the largest radio ministries in existence. Most ministries and churches can't do what he did because of the enormous expense. The payback on investment simply doesn't happen. Yet his efforts were effective.

One of the first times several of us visited Hank Hanegraaff at the Christian Research Institute, we were in the middle of having to decide, for financial reasons, whether *The World Tomorrow* television program should go off the air. Hank earnestly asked us not to let it die. "Clean up the doctrine," he said, "but you guys are one of the best programs on the air, getting to unchurched people a right idea of what Christianity is about. You're not a dog-and-pony show. At least if you continue your program with some changes, there will be somebody on the air with some measure of credibility." I think Herbert Armstrong can be credited with the high standards and professionalism that our program embodied.

On the print side of things, *The Plain Truth* began with Vol. I, No. 1 as a humble mimeographed paper on February 1, 1934, in order "to reach the world with the Gospel."[6] I'll let the former advertising man describe his own strategies:

God had been opening my mind to understanding of His truth. I had been experienced in magazine and newspaper writing. God put it in my mind to publish HIS magazine, making His TRUTH—the Bible—PLAIN, CLEAR, UNDERSTANDABLE, INTEREST-GRIPPING, DYNAMIC....

What I had in mind was articles dealing with world conditions and human interest problems—but always in the main content of the article, approaching that problem and dealing with it from the BIBLICAL revelation—so that in fact it was actually *making plain* the TRUTH—derived from *revelation*, not from science or secular scholarship of behavioral science and university-brand psychology....

Now, back to the BASIC POLICY and PURPOSE of *The Plain Truth*. I have already stated it—to make plain God's revealed TRUTH as it is in the Bible. To make the Bible *interesting!* To make it *understandable!* To make it COME ALIVE as a *NOW* Book!... We reach people 10 times more effectively through the eye than through the ear.[7]

The Plain Truth can and *must be* made the No. 1 MAGAZINE ON EARTH—utterly unique—no subscription price nor advertising revenue—making the biblical message not only plain but *dynamically interest-gripping, with a stronger public-reader appeal than even* Reader's Digest.

It must become the No. 1 *QUALITY* magazine, as a vigorous, dynamic, interest-grabbing magazine that literally makes God's truth *COME ALIVE!*...

We are the *only* voice in the wilderness of today's evils, frustrations, discouragements, with the world's ONLY HOPE—and its one SURE HOPE of happiness, abundance and eternal life!

We are going to develop the NEWSSTAND circulation into multiplied millions. But first, before I sell *The Plain Truth* to the newsstand audience, I must have a PRODUCT *that will grab attention, arouse instant interest, create suspense* and the DESIRE FOR MORE—AND MORE—AND MORE OF THE SAME![8]

After all these years, that still sounds like a strategy that would work, doesn't it? Mr. Armstrong was a master at causing readers and listeners to consider what the Bible had to say on current world and national issues. We can still learn much from him here. (And by the way, if you haven't seen the new *The Plain Truth*—now biblically accurate, doctrinally sound, captivating, challenging, and contemporary—give us a call at 1-800-309-4466.)

3. Concern over secular influences on young adults

One of the major concerns driving Mr. Armstrong to found Ambassador College was his desire to provide young people with a resource to combat harmful secular influences. One of the reasons he began writing back in the thirties was his antagonism toward atheistic evolution. He wasn't as informed on the subject as he might have been, but he was deeply concerned that atheism was negatively affecting the minds of young people and so took action. He was right on target in foreseeing how a purely secular outlook corrupts and eventually destroys the morals of a people and their nation.

4. Opposition to nominal Christianity

Mr. Armstrong took seriously the Bible's call to live out one's faith. He often preached against the kind of "faith" that would allow a person to disregard God's Word whenever it became convenient to do so. His concern reflects that of Paul in Acts 26:20:

First to those in Damascus, then to those in Jerusalem and in all Judea, and to the Gentiles also, I preached that they should repent and turn to God and prove their repentance by their deeds.

He was concerned that believers should honor God by obeying His divine commands. As Paul wrote in Romans: "What shall we say, then? Shall we go on sinning so that grace may increase? By no means! We died to sin; how can we live in it any longer?" (Romans 6:1–2). Mr. Armstrong took seriously the apostle's words in Titus about some professing believers: "They claim to know God, but by their actions they deny him. They are detestable, disobedient and unfit for doing anything good" (Titus 1:16). We now believe our founder's response to this legitimate concern was unbalanced, but that does not mean the concern itself was misguided. It still ought to be a concern for all of us.

5. Creation of a charitable foundation

Mr. Armstrong created the Ambassador Foundation, funded by the WCG, that he used to express his concern for impoverished and disadvantaged peoples around the world. Over the years he developed a special relationship with the people of Thailand, helping fund several agricultural and humanitarian projects in the country. Headlines from our internal newspaper, *The Worldwide News,* tell of numerous trips he made to Thailand, interacting with government officials and the nation's royalty. On January 22, 1984, the king of Thailand presented Mr. Armstrong with the Order of the White Elephant for his contributions to the welfare of his country. In February of the next year, Queen Sirikit of Thailand visited the United States to see Mr. Armstrong.

In retrospect it might be said that the foundation may have been overly generous in certain areas, but at least the right "heart" was present. It began to be acceptable for the church, through the foundation, to spend money on charitable works outside our own fellowship. We wouldn't do things in the same way today, but the foundation was a step in the right direction and away from our long isolation.

PROBLEMATIC AREAS

I should point out a few of the more personal doctrinal aberrations that affect my thinking about Mr. Armstrong. It is the existence of such problematic areas that cause me the most perplexity when I try to evaluate the ministry of our founder.

1. Who Is Elijah?

The very last text in the Old Testament reads: "See, I will send you the prophet Elijah before that great and dreadful day of the LORD comes. He will turn the hearts of the fathers to their children, and the hearts of the children to their fathers; or else I will come and strike the land with a curse" (Malachi 4:5–6).

Herbert Armstrong used to read Malachi 4:5–6 and say that it applied to him. One year before his death he published *Mystery of the Ages* in which he said:

> It is revealed in Malachi 3:1–5 and 4:5–6 that God would raise up one in the power and spirit of Elijah, shortly prior to the Second Coming of Christ. In Matthew 17:11 Jesus said, even after John the Baptist had completed his mission, that this prophesied Elijah "truly shall first come, and restore all things." Although it is plainly revealed that John the Baptist had come in the power and spirit of Elijah, he did not restore anything. The human leader to be raised up somewhat shortly prior to Christ's Second Coming was to prepare the way—prepare the Church—for Christ's coming, and restore the truth that had been lost through the preceding eras of the Church. Also a door was to be opened for this leader and/or the Philadelphia era of the Church to fulfill Matthew 24:14: "And this gospel of the kingdom shall be preached in all the world for a witness unto all nations; and then shall the end come."
>
> It was to be a time when, for the first time in the history of mankind, the weapons of mass destruction were produced that could erase all humanity from the earth (Matt. 24:21–22). This also was to occur just before the Second Coming of Christ (verses 29–30).
>
> These prophecies have now definitely been fulfilled. The true gospel has been restored and has now gone in power into every nation on the face of the earth.[9]

He was the Elijah who was going to come and turn the hearts of the fathers to their children and the hearts of the children to their fathers. He was the one who would prepare the way for the Second Coming of the Lord. Herbert Armstrong taught that he was the real fulfillment of this passage and that John the Baptist was merely an foreshadowing. Yet he had not always taught these things; the thought slowly evolved in his mind over the years.

At the beginning, people convinced Mr. Armstrong that we were doing an Elijah-like work because we were preparing the lost tribes of Israel for the Second Coming of Jesus. The lost tribes of Israel had lost their identity because they did not keep the Sabbath. Therefore, went the reasoning, Herbert Armstrong was restoring the Sabbath so that the lost tribes would understand their true heritage. Perhaps they would "wake up"—before it was too late.

After his first wife died and the idea started to play in Herbert Armstrong's mind—as his own ego accepted the notion and certain people began to play on his ego—he began to accept that he was *personally* the Elijah. This was part of the flirtation our church long has carried on with Old Testament personalities. We said we were the modern Ezekiel or the modern Zerubbabel or the modern (fill in the blank).

We have evidence in Herbert Armstrong's personal papers, that by 1929 he already believed he was called to give a unique prophetic vision to the world. This conviction came two years before his ordination and was tied in with the ideas of Anglo-Israelism, the Sabbath, and other Adventist doctrines he had come to accept. These beliefs helped set him up to later identify himself as the Elijah.

In the sixties we would say that WCG was doing an Elijah-like work. In the seventies we said that Herbert Armstrong himself was fulfilling the role of Elijah. Until the mideighties, Mr. Armstrong would consistently make statements such as this: "I have been asked, 'Are you the Elijah?' And I say, 'No.'"[10] Yet we already have seen what he said in *The Mystery of the Ages.* In the last two years of his life, in several sermons, he was even more explicit when he said directly, "I am Elijah." When Ron Kelly, one of our longtime ministers, heard Mr. Armstrong say this, he confessed to me, "I was alarmed when I heard him say, 'I am Elijah.' I could handle, 'I'm in the role of Elijah.' But 'I am Elijah'—what did he mean by that?"

As I look back, I wonder how in the world I did not question some of these claims: He was Elijah; he was Zerubbabel; he was given Ezekiel's commission. We taught that when the Book of Ezekiel was written, it was never delivered to its target audience, but that in these last days it finally was blossoming for us, its rightful readers. Of course, that makes absolutely no sense to me now, but it seemed right back then. Now I can clearly see that Herbert W. Armstrong was not another fulfillment of Elijah for two simple reasons:

- Mr. Armstrong has been dead for more than a decade; it is obvious he did not prepare the way for Christ's return; and
- Jesus himself taught that John the Baptist fulfilled Malachi's prophecy (Matthew 11:14).

2. The Evolution of an Apostle

Something very similar happened with Mr. Armstrong in his use of the term *apostle*. Although the ordination certificate he was issued in 1932 certified that "H. W. Armstrong is a recognized licensed minister, and apostle of the primitive faith," he didn't like the idea that he should be called an apostle. He wanted to be called superintendent or pastor or some other descriptive title. But in the 1950s his chief advisors said to him, "Mr. Armstrong, we have both evangelist-rank ministers and pastor-rank ministers. You need to be over all of The Work. You need to have apostolic authority over everyone. So being called apostle is a good thing." Mr. Armstrong relented and replied, in essence, "I'll accept this title as an ecclesiastical rank, but I'm not a New Testament apostle."

As time went on, however, Mr. Armstrong eventually became "the only true end-time apostle," or "Christ's Apostle," who received instruction directly from God through Christ. Over two or three decades he claimed rank on a par with the first-century apostles. Here is how he described his position in 1979:

When Christ chose His apostle for this time, he chose one who, 1) does *believe* what God says, 2) *will not* compromise or water down truths and doctrines Christ has given, and 3) has an OPEN MIND to receive further truth from Christ, and to be willing to acknowledge error when PROVED and turn from it! I do TREMBLE at the Word of God! I LOVE it, and I FEAR to go contrary to it or to mislead you, my brethren and my children in the Lord![11]

It is said that power corrupts and absolute power corrupts absolutely. Mr. Armstrong may have never wielded absolute power in our church, but by the same token, there weren't many who would challenge him on an issue. No doubt that is one reason why he earned a reputation "on the outside" as a theological despot. Sometime ago Mike Feazell, Greg Albrecht, and I were having lunch with several well-known, evangelical pastors. We were talking about our history and two of these men (who are now friends) joked with each other about their visiting Mr. Armstrong's formerly secluded offices. "Wow!" one said, "Could we sit in Herbert Armstrong's chair?" The other added, "Yeah! We could make a pronouncement or something."

I have little problem with a high church official using the title *apostle* to denote ecclesiastical rank within his denomination, but I do reject the idea that anyone today can legitimately be said to be an apostle on a par with the New Testament apostles. And in his heart of hearts, I think Mr. Armstrong did, too, as his comments regarding the publication of his *opus magnum* demonstrated.

3. The Publication of Mystery of the Ages

Herbert Armstrong considered the book *Mystery of the Ages* to be the great work of his life, the greatest book since the Bible. It was basically a compilation of scores of his magazine and church newspaper articles that had appeared through the years, organized into major topics. My father was among a group of a few trusted associates who helped Mr. Armstrong put the book together.

When the book was published in 1985, Mr. Armstrong addressed a class at

Ambassador College and handed out the book to sophomores and juniors, who were assigned to use it as a textbook. "This book is the greatest book since the Bible," he said, "and it was inspired just like the Bible." As he went on, he suddenly realized what he was saying, and you could almost see the wheels turning inside his head. He caught himself and started backpedaling. "I don't mean that this book is like the canon of Scripture," he said. "I don't mean that. I don't mean it was inspired like the Scripture was inspired." He didn't want anyone to put his book on the same level with Scripture. But why not, if he was an apostle on a par with the first-century apostles? I believe the answer is that he could never quite convince himself that he ranked as an equal with Paul and Peter and the rest of the New Testament apostles. He knew better.

Yet he was most definitely and absolutely in charge of our church. Herbert Armstrong was born in the nineteenth century and reflected the leadership style of the captains of industry. He looked up to Henry Ford and other great men like him. He admired the men who built the railroad and opened the banks. He wanted to be a great man. Since he didn't become a captain of industry in advertising, he ended up becoming a captain of religion. He embodied the entrepreneurial spirit, the pull-yourself-up-by-your-bootstraps attitude so necessary for a self-made man. His leadership style was definitely pre–World War II. He was the founder, and he came on the scene as this transcendental figure whom most of our members saw as having all authority and power, a man to whom members felt God spoke directly.

WHAT TO THINK?

Historical elements like these make it difficult for me to assess my own feelings about the ministry and leadership of Mr. Armstrong. While I will always be deeply grateful to him for instilling in me a profound respect for Scripture and a vital love of the Savior, I regret that we spent so many years majoring on minor and oftentimes aberrant issues. I have never felt that those years were wasted, but I do wish they had been spent much more productively. That ambivalence is also part of the legacy Mr. Armstrong left behind.

The legacy of the past can often be difficult, opening doors to emotion-filled closets and entryways to attics filled with skeletons and secrets. As the Worldwide Church of God has been dramatically changed and as we have faced the emotional upheaval of finding out much of what we believed was wrong, we have also had to face allegations about Herbert W. Armstrong and his son.

There is no question that his administrative and organizational structures allowed unbiblical teaching to be believed and perpetuated. In His mercy God has changed our doctrines first, and we are now working to change our governmental structure and polity.

There is a great deal of pain when longtime members are confronted with allegations about Herbert Armstrong or Garner Ted Armstrong. We not only lack the resources to verify or dismiss all such reports, we do not feel that God wants us to focus our energies on such things. Together with other leading administrators, I felt that we needed to apologize and ask forgiveness about our past unbiblical teaching and behavior.

While writing and editing these words, one of our church members directed an open letter on the Worldwide Web to me. Here are some excerpts from his posting in April 1997:

> I felt I needed to write this letter to you, hoping very much that you might be able to assuage the stress that I have felt and am feeling as a result of unearthing some rather distasteful and upsetting information through the Worldwide Web. Perhaps I could even go as far as terming it a "crisis of confidence and trust," not unlike the feeling that I imagine I might experience if a longtime friend would suddenly turn around and tell me that I don't matter all that much to him or her after all? A feeling of betrayal, confusion, sadness, anger, bewilderment? In short, a feeling of grief?… Openness and honesty; this is what I am asking of you now in this letter. The point is this: we need the truth. People want the truth. What really did go on in the Worldwide Church of God hierarchy? Was there abuse? If so, what kind? Who were the perpetrators? Was anything

done about it? If so, what? If not, why not?... It was thoroughly disturbing to discover that so much went on in the church that I had no idea of because it was kept from the membership. I felt cheated, used and profoundly disappointed.

Yours sincerely,

Here is the response I sent on May 6, 1997:

Please accept this letter as a response to the open letter you posted on the World Wide Web on April 26, 1997. You stated that the posting was largely as a result of "unearthing some rather distasteful and upsetting information through the Worldwide Web."

Your posting describes your emotional reactions with words like "betrayal," "confusion," "sadness," "anger" and "bewilderment." While I am not specifically aware of what you "unearthed," I do have a general sense of the kinds of issues you may have seen and read. During the past few years we in the Worldwide Church of God have been attempting to give gracious answers regarding allegations about past leaders of the church while we have been responding to what God has been teaching us.

We have attempted to avoid "bashing Mr. Armstrong," his son or other past leaders for either real or alleged misconduct and behavior. On the other hand, we have clearly asked forgiveness of our members, former members, readers of The Plain Truth and those who listened to us on the radio and watched our television program. In case you did not see them originally, I am enclosing the "Personal" from The Plain Truth for both February 1996 ("A Church Reborn") and from March/April 1996 ("Forgive Us Our Trespasses").

We have not mentioned names or personalities or specific sins, problems or allegations. We have offered sincere, heart-felt apologies for the teaching, practice and behaviors of the historic Worldwide Church of God. Even our careful attempts to present facts about how we have been wrong in the past have resulted in angry and bitter accusations of

"Armstrong bashing." Virtually all of the individuals who were primarily responsible for authoritarian approaches and extravagant lifestyles are either deceased or have long since left our fellowship to join splinter groups that continue to proclaim some degree of teaching associated with Herbert W. Armstrong.

We do not believe that it is our Christian duty to unearth and expose—even if it were possible—to find out the "truth." There is much discussion, supposition and allegation about the past. We know some of it to be true, assume some of it is supposition, while some is fabrication. What we can do now is to move on and be the kind of church, and the kind of Christians, who do not engage in such unbiblical teaching, behavior or practices. God has not asked us to be the judge of Mr. Armstrong, his son or others who held high administrative positions in the historic Worldwide Church of God. Of course, we have judged his unbiblical teachings and have changed them.

We neither have nor promote an extravagant lifestyle. We have divested ourselves, and continue to, of those things that are opulent and do not befit a church. We have "come clean" as you request. A few months ago I wrote a letter to all members of the Worldwide Church of God letting them know that every employee of the church has a salary which is less than $100,000 per year. In case you did not see that letter, I am enclosing a copy.

We give thanks to God that he is beginning to heal the hurts and wounds not only within our fellowship, but within churches and people worldwide. God is working to bring about reconciliation—the reconciliation that is possible because of the finished work of Christ on the cross. We are committed to continuing to heal and to bind up the wounds and to work for unity within the body of Christ, rather than division.

In Christ's service,

Joseph Tkach

As I said at the beginning of this chapter, I know there are some readers who want me to condemn Herbert W. Armstrong as a heretic. There are others who want me to lionize him as the greatest man of God since the apostle Paul. So where do I stand today?

First, I firmly believe that as a church we were essentially wrong on many crucial issues—and yet I also know that it was Mr. Armstrong who put the system in place that eventually got us where we are today. While much of what Mr. Armstrong taught was in serious error, he also gave us some things—a profound respect for the Bible, for example—that helped to pave the way to our current biblical understandings.

Second, I could point out that many men God has used did a lot of foolish things or made many inaccurate or even harmful statements. All of us show our brokenness in one way or another. John Wesley was not known for having an ideal marriage. Martin Luther was stridently anti-Semitic. John Calvin allowed a theological opponent to be burned at the stake. It's not my place (or yours) to question their standing in Christ. The same could be said of Mr. Armstrong.

Please don't ask me to make a decision on his soul; that's not my prerogative, nor is it yours. On this issue I think of the Lord's response to Peter when, after the latter heard a disturbing personal prophecy, he turned toward the apostle John and demanded of Jesus, "Lord, what about him?" Jesus replied in no uncertain terms, "What is that to you? You must follow me" (John 21:21–22). That remains a good word for us today.

I'd like to close this chapter with a story. A little while ago some of us had lunch with a well-known evangelical leader and author. Toward the end of our time together he said something incredible for us in the Worldwide Church of God. "Let me tell you where I am on this thing," he said. "I think that when your dad gave that sermon on Christmas Eve, God was tapping Herbert Armstrong on the shoulder and saying, 'Take a look at this—I want to show you something.' And I think Herbert Armstrong was leading the cheers when your dad introduced the new covenant to the Worldwide Church of God."

I like the sound of that. I like it a whole lot.

FROM ETERNITY TO HERE

A s I close this book I'd like to address two separate audiences and then give my personal assessment as to where our church is and where it's headed.

A WORD TO THOSE WITH AN UNANSWERED QUESTION

Repeatedly in the past few years I have been asked by many WCG members, "How could God have allowed us to wander in serious error for thirty or forty or even fifty years? Where was He all that time?"

My answer is this: It's really not God's fault. He's not to blame. He's not the one culpable for our ignorance, for our lack of scholarship, for our mistakes in interpreting Scripture. All those things were our own doing. We fell into false-hood because of our brokenness, because we are people born in sin, because we tried to manage things on our own.

God has known all the time that we have been doctrinally off the track. Yet God is sovereign, and He is infinitely greater than our sin and confusion and errors. In His sovereignty and love He has been patient with us. Today I have a deeper appreciation than ever before for the apostle's words: "The Lord is not slow in keeping his promise, as some understand slowness. He is patient with you, not want-ing anyone to perish, but everyone to come to repentance" (2 Peter 3:9).

The Bible tells us that God orchestrates earthly events to fulfill His holy will, and in our case He has chosen to *slowly* move us from error (heterodoxy) into truth (orthodoxy). I don't blame Him for that; I think that gives Him great glory!

From everything I can understand, what has happened within our body is unique and unprecedented. It's not due to anything we've done. If anything, our involvement has often served only to mess things up. Anything good or note-worthy that has happened among us is to God's credit. Many times we have said, "He has done this in spite of us, not because of us."

When you stop to think about it, the question, "Why did God allow us to remain in such error?" could be asked many times over of people and situations in the Bible itself. Why did God allow Cain to kill Abel? Why did He allow Eve to take the forbidden fruit? Why did He allow Abraham to offer his wife to pagan kings, not once but twice? Why did He allow Paul and Barnabas to get into such a big fight that they split up their missionary team? Why did He allow Peter to deny the Lord Jesus three times? Why did He allow Judas to betray Christ? Why? Why? Why?

Isn't it amazing that God always seems to come on the scene about a minute too late? Why does He do that?

I think He does this because He wants people to seek Him out of the deep desire of their hearts, not merely because they have no choice. God could have prevented Eve from eating the forbidden fruit; He could have appeared to her in front of the tree before she took her first bite and said, "My dear, didn't I tell you not to eat from this tree? Now give me that and run along." He could have pre-vented Cain from killing his brother. He could have prevented so many things that He did not. Why? Because He has given us the ability to choose freely what we will do, and sadly, much of what we choose is not good.

Now that God has led us into greater understanding of His Word and His will, what will we do? I recommend that we listen carefully to the words of Jere-miah the prophet, then act on them: "'For I know the plans I have for you,' declares the LORD, 'plans to prosper you and not to harm you, plans to give you hope and a future. Then you will call upon me and come and pray to me, and I will listen to you. You will seek me and find me when you seek me with all your heart'" (Jeremiah 29:11–13).

We must continue to seek God with all of our heart. When we seek Him from the heart, He discloses Himself to us. Already we have seen Him fulfill this word to us—perhaps not in the timing we would like, but faithfully nonetheless. My recommendation is that we continue to seek His face. If the first part of our journey has proven so life giving, who can tell what lies ahead?

A WORD TO OUR NEW FRIENDS

To the greater Christian community, I would ask that you continue to pray for us as we find our way in the body of Christ. Continue to rejoice with us in what God has done, and continue to delight in God's glory as He faithfully leads all of us together into greater conformity to the image of His dear Son.

One of the nice things that happens when parents have a new baby is the outburst of joy expressed by other members of the family. Have you ever heard women comparing labor stories? They're not happy about the pain, but they are excited about the new birth. It's something to celebrate. As Jesus said, "A woman giving birth to a child has pain because her time has come; but when her baby is born she forgets the anguish because of her joy that a child is born into the world. So with you: Now is your time of grief, but I will see you again and you will rejoice, and no one will take away your joy" (John 16:21–22). Jesus spoke these words shortly before his arrest and crucifixion. He intended them to comfort his disciples during the agonizing moments that would soon follow.

That seems to be a frequent biblical pattern: words of a promise, followed by pain, followed by joy. "Weeping may remain for a night," says the psalmist, "but rejoicing comes in the morning" (Psalm 30:5).

In the past few years we have learned quite a bit about the reality of this pattern. Our changes have come at great cost. Church leadership continues to receive angry and even threatening letters. Family members consider us demon-possessed or worse. There are Christians who are skeptical of the miraculous transformation brought about by God. While we certainly understand from a human perspective, it is sad that there are believers unwilling to forgive the prac-tical implications of our past teaching.

There has been weeping in the night, yet rejoicing does come in the morning! Despite the pain, despite the sleepless nights and new problems that continue to pop up, we can truly say it's been worth it all. I can say with Paul: "Whatever was to my profit I now consider loss for the sake of Christ. What is more, I consider everything a loss compared to the surpassing greatness of knowing Christ Jesus my Lord, for whose sake I have lost all things. I consider them rubbish, that I may gain Christ and be found in him, not having a righteousness of my own that comes from the law, but that which is through faith in Christ—the righteousness that comes from God and is by faith" (Philippians 3:7–9).

And so my final word to you, my brothers and sisters in Christ, is this: Rejoice with us in the glory of God!

WHAT LIES AHEAD?

The last line from an article on the Worldwide Church of God in George Mather's *Dictionary of Cults, Sects, Religions and the Occult* says this: "The story of what the WCG will have to offer once all of the dust has settled remains to be seen."[1] Those words were written in 1993, but the statement remains valid. Many things still remain unclear about what our church ultimately will look like. This should not be surprising; the New Testament itself shows us that major change often takes time.

The apostle Paul, after his encounter with Christ on the road to Damascus, immediately began to preach that Jesus is the Son of God (Acts 9:20). Yet it took some time for him to be accepted into Christian fellowship. The Christians in Jerusalem were understandably skeptical of him—after all, this was the brute who had hauled them out of their homes and thrown them into prison, if he didn't get them stoned first—and it took a bridge builder named Barnabas to bring him into the group (vv. 26–27). Not long thereafter, Paul was sent to Tarsus (v. 30).

God had great plans for Paul, but it took many years for those plans to be fully implemented. Paul spent three years in Arabia and many more in Tarsus. What he preached and whom he reached during that period, we do not know. But it must have given Paul time to clarify his thoughts. He had heard the arguments of the early Christians; he knew well the arguments of the Jews who did not believe. No doubt he used his "preparation time" to formulate his own arguments that Jesus was in fact the long-prophesied Messiah.

Yet he was not alone. Paul soon received help from his newfound Christian friends. He already knew what they were teaching, and they taught him more—yet he still had questions to think about. Why did the Messiah have to die? Why did the Jews not accept the Messiah whom God had given them? Where had the Jewish religion led them astray? If one could be right with God under Old Covenant laws, then why did God have to send His Son to die? Paul had to think through all the implications of his new faith, thoughts we would later read in his epistles.

From the beginning, God had chosen Paul to be a missionary to the Gentiles (see Acts 9:15). Yet Paul was forced to wait in the wings for many years. The way Luke tells the story, Paul wasn't even around when the first Gentiles came into the church (Acts 10). Paul doesn't really enter the picture until after many Gentiles already had become part of the church at Antioch (Acts 11:20–26). And it was only after some time in Antioch that Paul actually began doing the work for which Christ had called him.

I see many parallels between the story of Paul and the story of the Worldwide Church of God. We both have roots in the Old Covenant. We both have embraced the New with joy. For both of us there have been Barnabas-like people who have helped reconcile us to other Christians and who have helped teach us. And it has taken us both some time to understand our identity and our role in the Christian world. (It took many years for the church as a whole to make a full transition from a worship rooted in the Old Testament to a faith based in the New Covenant.)

Of course, we have no delusions of grandeur that we will have the impact of the apostle Paul! We do not entertain the notion that we will turn the world upside down.

Yet we do expect God to use us to preach the gospel of Jesus Christ. Perhaps there is a niche out there that needs our particular experience. Perhaps God is preparing us for situations that do not yet exist. We do not know what lies ahead, but we remain ready to respond to God's leading.

WHY CONTINUE TO EXIST?

When our foundational doctrines were changed, some people suggested the Worldwide Church of God should just close its doors and tell its members to start attending healthy, authentic Christian churches. Ironically, we heard this not from Christians in other churches, but from a few of our own members! They were angry and bitter, believing that the WCG had caused such pain in their lives by teaching erroneous doctrines. I think that a few hoped that we had "shot ourselves in the foot." They concluded that the WCG had been built on false pretenses and therefore had no right to exist.

We acknowledge that our historic, unbiblical doctrines were in error. We further acknowledge that the WCG would never have come into existence without those erroneous doctrines. But we do not conclude from those facts that Jesus Christ rescued us as a group merely to have us disband. He has bought and paid for this church. It belongs to Him and we have told Him that He can do with it whatever pleases Him. If it is of any value to Him, He can use it as His instrument. We are happy to let Him lead us, wherever that may be. We rejoice in the fellowship we have with Him, and we believe He is already leading us into usefulness.

There's a second reason we do not believe it is God's will that we dissolve: Our shared experiences mean that we have things we need to learn as a group, things we will not learn if we disband. We also hope that, by God's grace, our shared experiences give us something to teach. And who will be our students? Our primary mission field right now is our own members. Some of them have not accepted the doctrinal changes. Many who have accepted them have not yet begun to integrate them into their life and faith. This must be our primary focus for the immediate future.

As a group, we are enjoying a new interest in and appreciation for worship. We are discovering our spiritual gifts and the power of lay ministry. We are learning to function in new ways.

Our strengths as a denomination include a high respect for Scripture and a willingness to do what it says. We recognize that Jesus, our Savior and our Lord, instructs us about how to think, how to speak, and how to act. We know that Christ makes an enormous difference in the way we live. He transforms our lives in this age, even as He gives us eternal life for the ages to come. We stress prayer and Bible study as important aspects of spiritual growth. Our recent history gives us a deep longing for grace and a wariness toward legalism.

Even so, we are well aware that there is much for us to learn, even as we teach. Because of our hostility toward traditional Christianity, few of our pastors have had seminary training. Events of the past few years have forced us to study a great deal on specific issues, but we need to broaden our educational base. In response we have instituted training programs for our pastors, including our lay pastors. We are thankful for the help that many Barnabas-like Christians have eagerly given us.

Several significant concerns still face us. One concerns our chosen day of worship. Some members, upon learning that the New Covenant does not command the seventh-day Sabbath, concluded that it was a sin for us to continue meeting on Saturdays. But in most cases, we will serve our members best by continuing to meet on Saturdays. The New Covenant does not require us to switch to Sunday. Paul might say to us, "Each one should be fully convinced in his own mind" (Romans 14:5).

Many of our members have arranged to have time off on Saturdays; some work on Sundays. Others find Saturday less convenient, but are willing to meet then because other members cannot attend at other times. Some members who do not yet understand the doctrinal change would simply refuse to meet on any other day. If we hope to teach such people, we must meet on the day they will listen. For a variety of reasons, then, most of our congregations still meet on Saturdays. A few of our congregations have begun to meet on Sunday.

Another issue: Our annual festivals have been questioned, since they were based on Old Covenant festivals and the Hebrew calendar. The New Covenant does not require these days, but neither does it require us to stop their observance. The first century Jerusalem Christians apparently continued observing these festivals for many years. For Christians today, these festivals are optional. Most of our members still wish to observe them, so we gather and enjoy another opportunity to hear the gospel preached! We now use these annual festivals as celebrations of salvation:

- The Passover has become a celebration of the Lord's Supper, in memory of Christ, our Passover (1 Corinthians 5:7).
- The Festival of Unleavened Bread reminds us that Christ has brought us out of the slavery of sin and we serve him as instruments of righteousness, sincerity, and truth (1 Corinthians 5:7–8).
- Pentecost commemorates the Holy Spirit, given that we might be transformed into the image of Christ and be witnesses of what Jesus has done in our lives.
- The Festival of Trumpets reminds us that our Savior will return, and we will all be resurrected to live with Him.
- The Day of Atonement celebrates Jesus' death to atone for our sins.
- The Festival of Tabernacles reminds us that the greatest blessings are yet to come in a future much more wonderful than we could possibly imagine.

For decades, we prejudiced our members against Christmas and Easter by teaching that they originated as pagan days of worship. We have explained that our line of reasoning was wrong—yet for some members, the stigma remains. No doubt this will fade in time, but right now, these holidays do not have a high profile with everyone in the Worldwide Church of God. There is no biblical command that we observe these days, so we strive to be sensitive to our members' concerns. At the same time, many members find great joy in celebrating Christmas and Easter, and we share in their joy. This year we had Resurrection Sunday services in many of our congregations for the first time. And an increasingly larger percentage of our membership is celebrating the birth of Jesus.

Our denominational governance is yet another major change we are in the process of making. The hierarchy of church structure is being modified to feature a board vested with authority both to appoint and to remove the president/pastor general. We also plan to limit the length of the pastor general's term to a specified number of years. Until now, the office of pastor general has been a lifetime appointment made by the previous pastor general. We expect these changes to be effective by the end of 1997 or early 1998.

Another of our immediate challenges is finances. Our membership has dropped by half, but our income has dropped much more than that. The theological foundations on which we formerly gathered money were flawed, so it is no surprise that members now give less than they used to. Many members are still confused by the doctrinal changes and are understandably reluctant to support reforms they don't understand.

Our financial limitations have caused us to terminate the employment of some pastors, to cancel our mass-media evangelism, to greatly cut back on our teaching materials, and to reduce other expenses. Meanwhile, we are burdened with the maintenance costs on properties we no longer use. Those properties have been put up for sale, but until they sell, we face significant budgetary difficulties.

We are well aware that our income may not improve until members come to understand New Covenant Christianity, become comfortable with the doctrinal changes, and find joy in and enthusiasm about the church they attend. Congregations need to heal internally before new people can be adequately nurtured in the faith. All of this takes time.

Few of our congregations own their own buildings, but this is probably a good thing, since it means we are not saddled with mortgages for buildings larger than needed.

So where do we go from here? I believe the Lord Jesus will show us the way. He has brought us this far, and He has promised to take us the rest of the way.

"He who began a good work in you will carry it on to completion until the day of Christ Jesus" (Philippians 1:6). Our legitimacy comes from Jesus, the author and finisher of our faith.

As I conclude these words in early May 1997, we have just received a press release from the National Association of Evangelicals. Its first two sentences read: "The Board of Directors of the National Association of Evangelicals (NAE) has voted overwhelmingly to accept the Worldwide Church of God (WCG), head-quartered in Pasadena, California, into membership. The application process included examination of doctrinal changes which have taken place in the once-controversial denomination."

What has happened among us in the Worldwide Church of God is a testament to God's infinite grace and His sovereignty over eternity. We can take no credit. Our church has been claimed and redeemed by our merciful Savior, and He is still shaping us for His purpose. By His grace, may we be found to be useful servants in His kingdom.

NOTES

CHAPTER TWO: CHRISTMAS EVE SERMON, 1994

1. Michael Morrison, "Case Study: Doctrinal Change and Denominational Schism," unpublished paper for Church Leadership and Administration class at C. P. Haggard School of Theology, Azusa Pacific University, November 10, 1996, 4.

CHAPTER THREE: MY PILGRIMAGE

1. Philip Yancey, *The Jesus I Never Knew* (Grand Rapids, Mich.: Zondervan Publishing House, 1995), 23, 25.

CHAPTER FOUR: THE RIGHT HAND OF FELLOWSHIP

1. David Neff, "The Road to Orthodoxy," *Christianity Today,* October 2, 1995, 15.
2. Ruth Tucker, "From the Fringe to the Fold: How the Worldwide Church of God discovered the plain truth of the gospel," *Christianity Today,* July 15, 1996, 26–27.
3. Ibid., 27.
4. Doug LeBlanc, "The Worldwide Church of God: Resurrected into Orthodoxy," *The Christian Research Journal* (winter 1996): 7.
5. Tucker, "From the Fringe," 29.
6. LeBlanc, "Resurrected into Orthodoxy," 7.
7. "New Beginning, New Leadership for Worldwide Church of God," *Christian Research Newsletter* 9, no. 1 (winter/spring 1996): 13.
8. Tucker, "From the Fringe," 32.
9. Letter to the Editor, *Charisma,* March 1997, 9.
10. Tucker, "From the Fringe," 32.

CHAPTER SIX: A SERVANT OF THE PEOPLE

1. Stanley R. Rader, "The Attorney General Kept His Word. Now I Will Keep Mine," *The Worldwide News,* March 6, 1981, special edition, 9.
2. Herbert W. Armstrong, "CONGRESS OF LEADING MINISTERS HEARS DEFINED AND REEMPHASIZED SPIRITUAL ORGANIZATION OF CHURCH," *The Worldwide News,* March 6, 1981, special edition, 12.

CHAPTER SEVEN: WHAT WE BELIEVED

1. There is no copyright on Herbert W. Armstrong's first edition of *The United States and the British Commonwealth in Prophecy,* probably because it is so similar to J. H. Allen's book.
2. *The Worldwide News,* May 21, 1979, 1.
3. *The Worldwide News,* November 16, 1981. 1.
4. *The Worldwide News,* December 28, 1981. 1.
5. Herbert W. Armstrong, *The Good News,* November 20, 1978, 5.
6. Ibid.

7. Ibid., 4.

8. Armstrong, "CONGRESS OF LEADING MINISTERS," 10.

9. Herbert W. Armstrong, "Just What Is the Work?" *The Worldwide News,* June 30, 1980, 1.

10. John Robinson, "How WCG's Top-Down Rule Evolved," *In Transition,* December 16, 1996, 7.

11. *The Good News,* December 18, 1978, 5.

12. Robinson, "Top-Down Rule," 7.

13. Ibid.

14. Herbert W. Armstrong, "The Plain Truth about the Covenants," *The Good News,* December 18, 1978, 1, 8.

15. Herbert W. Armstrong, "Non-tithing Is Stealing," *The Worldwide News,* July 9, 1979, 1, 5.

16. Herbert W. Armstrong, "AND NOW CHRIST SETS CHURCH BACK ON TRACK DOCTRINALLY!" *The Worldwide News,* special edition, February 19, 1979, 2.

17. Herbert W. Armstrong, "SEVEN PROOFS OF THE TRUE CHURCH," *The Good News,* November 20, 1978, 16.

CHAPTER EIGHT: THE FIRST REFORMS

1. Herbert W. Armstrong, *Does God Heal Today?* (Pasadena, Calif.: Radio Church of God, 1952), 2.

2. Ibid.

3. Ibid, 6.

4. Ibid, 9–10.

5. Ibid., 11.

6. Ibid., 15.

7. Herbert W. Armstrong, *The Plain Truth about Healing* (Pasadena, Calif.: The Worldwide Church of God, 1979), 67.

8. Ibid., 69.

9. Ibid., 49–50.

10. Joseph W. Tkach, "New Understanding of the Meaning of Christ's Broken Body and the Church's Teaching on HEALING," *The Worldwide News,* March 23, 1987, 3.

11. Ibid., 4.

12. Ibid.

13. Ibid.

14. Ibid., 5.

15. Herbert W. Armstrong, "How subtly Satan used MAKEUP to start the Church off the track," *The Worldwide News,* November 16, 1981, 1, 4–5.

CHAPTER NINE: THE CENTRAL PLANK CRACKS

1. Herbert W. Armstrong, *Which Day Is the Christian Sabbath?* (Pasadena, Calif.: The Worldwide Church of God, 1976), 41–42.

2. Ibid., 44.

3. Ibid., 44–45.

4. *Study Paper: How Anglo-Israelism Entered the Churches of God, The Worldwide Church of God,* November 1995, 3.

5. Ibid., 4.

6. Ibid., 9.

7. Ibid., 9–10.

8. Ibid., 10.

9. Ibid., 2.

10. Ibid., 19–20.

11. Ibid., 14.

12. Ibid., 12.

13. Ibid., 13.

14. Ibid., 14.

15. Ibid., 18.

16. Ibid., 19.

17. Armstrong, *Which Day Is the Christian Sabbath?* 35.

18. Ibid., 37.

19. Ibid., 39.

20. Ibid., 44.

21. *Study Paper: United States and Britain in Prophecy, The Worldwide Church of God,* November 1995, 2–3.

22. In February 1997 we filed suit against the Philadelphia Church of God—one of our splinter groups headquartered in Edmund, Oklahoma—to block the republication of *Mystery of the Ages.* The Worldwide Church of God still holds the copyright to this book, and we contend that no one else has the right to publish it. We feel it is our Christian duty to keep this book out of print, not because we recognize "the power and clarity of Mr. Armstrong's vision" or because our church "lacks confidence in the appeal of its own muddled and compromised approach," as an advertisement for the Philadelphia church claims, but because we believe Mr. Armstrong's doctrinal errors are better left out of circulation.

23. *Study Paper: The United States and Britain in Prophecy,* 1–2.

CHAPTER TEN: WHAT'S ALL THIS "JESUS STUFF"?

1. Herbert W. Armstrong, "SEVEN PROOFS OF THE TRUE CHURCH," *The Good News,* December 4, 1978, 11.

2. Herbert W. Armstrong, "THE WORLDWIDE CHURCH OF GOD TODAY," *The*

Good News, December 18, 1978, 5.

3. Herbert W. Armstrong, "THE GREAT MAJESTIC GOD being enthroned in eyes of Church once again by Jesus Christ," *The Good News,* July 31, 1978, 1.

4. Herbert W. Armstrong, "WHAT YOU MAY NOT KNOW!" *The Good News,* July 31, 1978, 4.

5. Personal letter to Joseph Tkach Sr., dated March 6, 1995. Name withheld for reasons of confidentiality.

6. David Hulme, *New Beginnings,* June 16, 1995.

7. Herbert W. Armstrong, "SEVEN PROOFS OF THE TRUE CHURCH," *The Good News,* November 20, 1978, 4.

8. Ibid., 5.

CHAPTER ELEVEN: HOW COULD WE
HAVE BELIEVED THESE THINGS?

1. Dennis Coon, *Introduction to Psychology: Exploration and Application,* 3d ed. (St. Paul, Minn.: West Publishing Company, 1983), 588.

2. Armstrong, "CONGRESS OF LEADING MINISTERS," 2.

3. Herbert W. Armstrong, *The Good News,* August 28, 1978, 1.

4. Ibid., 7.

5. Herbert W. Armstrong, "A WHOLE NEW BALL GAME," *The Worldwide News,* January 28, 1980, 1.

6. Ibid., 12.

7. Herbert W. Armstrong, "COMPLETION OF WORK NEAR???" *The Worldwide News,* June 16, 1980, 1.

8. Herbert W. Armstrong, "SATAN INTENSIFIES PERSECUTION," *The Worldwide News,* June 16, 1980, 1.

9. Herbert W. Armstrong, "THE PRESIDENTIAL CAMPAIGN," *The Worldwide News,* June 30, 1980, 5.

10. Armstrong, "CONGRESS OF LEADING MINISTERS," 1.

11. Ibid., 2.

12. Coon, *Introduction to Psychology,* 584.

13. Roderick C. Meredith, *The Plain Truth,* August 1957.

14. Roderick C. Meredith, *The Plain Truth,* December 1963.

15. Roderick C. Meredith, *The Plain Truth,* February 1965.

16. Garner Ted Armstrong, *Twentieth Century Watch: News Flash,* February 15, 1997.

17. Herbert W. Armstrong, "SEVEN PROOFS OF THE TRUE CHURCH," *The Good News,* November 20, 1978, 4.

18. Ibid.

CHAPTER TWELVE: THE ENIGMA OF HERBERT W. ARMSTRONG

1. While the popular understanding in our church long has been that Mr. Armstrong came to his Sabbatarian convictions as a direct result of Loma's challenge to him, notes written by Mr. Armstrong (probably in the late '20s) indicate this may not be accurate. In one, a draft note to A. N. Dugger written on the back of preprinted stationery ("Survey of Laundry Conditions"), Mr. Armstrong says of the Sabbath question, "In a word, Mr. Dugger, my present status on the question is just this: It now appears to me that the Bible says the Sabbath is abolished, ended, and done away. That, so far as Divine Command is concerned, there IS NO SABBATH." Later in that same note he indicates he was already teaching that believers should keep the Sabbath when he writes, "We do it [i.e., keep the Sabbath] because we WANT to keep it, and not because we feel God COMMANDS us to keep it. But you see, Mr. Dugger, feeling as I do about it, now, I cannot write or speak to others on the question. And I am perplexed as to what should be my course regarding those present. I am merely keeping silent so far as they are concerned, and they do not know of my present perplexity. If I become finally convinced I have misled them, I shall most certainly make every effort within my power to undo what I have done.

"Of course this does not need to prevent any usefulness I might have in reaching others with God's message. Sabbath keeping, in ANY event, will not bring salvation. The Sabbath question is a minor one compared to the paramount question of salvation—yet I think it important, as it affects RETENTION of salvation.

"Sooner or later, this question will be cleared up for me. The real truth will be revealed to me, whichever it is. I have prayed earnestly for it, and it is God's promise that a prayer of that kind is going to be answered. Perhaps you can be a means of helping me get it cleared up. It seems to me the truth OUGHT to be on the side of the question I know you believe.

"But, Mr. Dugger, even believing as I know you do, how would you answer one like my sister who said to me 'I have prayed and prayed, earnestly, for the Lord to tell me if He wanted me to keep Saturday for the Sabbath, but I have never felt I should do it. If I have been converted, and come to Jesus and repented, and accepted Him as my Saviour, and tried earnestly to live according to everything He taught, and yet don't keep Saturday for the Sabbath, when no one was ever commanded to keep that day but the Jews between Moses and Christ—I can't feel I am wrong because I don't do something Jesus never said to do, nor any of the Apostles!' The New Testament, my sister reminded me, says that if we repent and 'believe on the Lord Jesus Christ, you shall be saved.' How would you answer her?

"Trusting you will be able to help me, I am, Very sincerely,"

What appears to be a "working document" by Mr. Armstrong, from approximately the same period, says this: "Paul said we are not under the law. I have studied this from every possible angle, and tried every possible interpretation. And I cannot persuade myself that the plain, obvious meaning Paul intended to give us by that statement was anything except that we are not under obligation to obey the Mosaic Law, including the Ten Commandments.... Paul's writings, in other words, appear to confirm the idea that God's Law means supreme love to God and equal love to one's fellows, and not specifically the Ten Commandments at all. Paul's writings seem to convincingly indicate that the Law of God, in effect BEFORE Sinai, was those Two Great Commandments, and not the Ten Commandments. In that case, until the Ten Commandments were given the Jews, there was no command to keep the Sabbath, and when the Ten Commandments went, at the Cross, the Sabbath obligation went again, and then there remained just what had existed before—the Two Great Commandments, which, by themselves, give no thought or even suggestion of any Sabbath.... And so it goes. I am frankly undecided. The Bible does not clearly settle the question. Positive direct proof, I believe, is not given in Scripture.... Personally, I am in doubt, and while in doubt, shall continue to play safe by observing Saturday. But, being in doubt, I *cannot* set myself up as a teacher on the subject. The subject is simply bewildering."

2. Herbert W. Armstrong, "Editor's Note," *The Good News,* June 5, 1978, 1.

3. Herbert W. Armstrong, "Would You Accuse Jesus Christ?" *The Worldwide News,* November 12, 1979, 3.

4. Armstrong, "CHURCH BACK ON TRACK," 1.

5. Ibid.

6. Armstrong, "Editor's Note," 1.

7. Herbert W. Armstrong, "And NOW—The PLAIN TRUTH being Set Back on Track," *The Good News,* September 11, 1978, 1.

8. Ibid., 6.

9. Herbert W. Armstrong, *The Mystery of the Ages* (Pasadena, Calif.: The Worldwide Church of God, 1985), 290–1.

10. Armstrong, "CONGRESS OF LEADING MINISTERS," 10.

11. Armstrong, "CHURCH BACK ON TRACK," 4.

EPILOGUE: FROM ETERNITY TO HERE

1. George Mather and Larry A. Nichols, *Dictionary of Cults, Sects, Religions and the Occult* (Grand Rapids, Mich.: Zondervan Publishing House, 1993), 325.

Worldwide Church of God Organizational Splits

1937   Radio Church of God (Herbert W. Armstrong)
            1968   Worldwide Church of God (Herbert W. Armstrong)
                     1986   Joseph W. Tkach
                            1995   Joseph Tkach

1970   Church of God (Carl O'Beirn)...............
*   Top of the Line (John Kerley).................
*   Restoration Church of God (M. John Allen)................
*   Church of God Boise City, Oklahoma (B. Ballew & V. Cryer)..............
*   Sabbatarian (Marvin Faulhaber)...............
1970   Fountain of Life Fellowship (James & Virginia Porter)................
1972   Restoration Fellowship (Sir Anthony Buzzard)................
1972   The Total Truth (Lee Grose)................
1973   Church of God Seventh Era (Larry Gilbert Johnson)_____
1973   Church of God Shreveport (John Mitchell)_____
1974   Baltimore Church of God (Dan Porter)................
1974   Great Lakes Society for Biblical Research (John Cheetam)................

1974   Foundation for Biblical Research (E. Martin, G. Arvidson & K. Fisher)_____→
            1984   Association for Scriptural Knowledge (E. Martin)_____→
                  1992   The Association for Biblical Christians (Dallas James)................
            1979   World Insight (G. Arvidson & K. Storey)................

1974   Associated Churches, Inc. (Ken Westby & George Kemnitz)_____→
            1978   United Church of God (Richard Wiedenheft)_____
            1983   Family of God (John Shirn)................

1975   Song in the Night (Cecil Battles)_____→

1975   Church of God Eternal (Raymond Cole)_____→
            1976   Church of God Sonoma (Paul Royer)_____→
            1978   Giving and Sharing Ministry (Richard Nickels)_____→
            1980   Bible Study Association (Davis Northnagel)_____→

1975   Universal Church of God (Ray Lampley)_____→
1975   Emissary Publications (Des Griffen)................
1975   Religion in the News (William Hinson)................
1975   Liberty Foundation (Al Carrozzo)................
1976   Seek and Find Ministries of the Church of El Shaddai (Ray Stapleton)_____→
1978   Church of God Churchlight Publishing Association (Jack Hines)_____→
1978   Family Church of God (Rick Gipe)................
1978   Mystery of the Kingdom Ministry (Martin Muzynoski)_____→

1978   Church of God International (Garner Ted Armstrong)_____
              *   Assembly of God in Christ Jesus (Bill Phillips)_____→
              *   Disciples Church of God (Clyde Holman)................
              *   Church of the Savior at Cincinnati (Cliff Robertson)................
            1979   The Pure Truth (Richard Scott)................
            1980   Church of God Evangelistic Association (Dave Smith)_____→

	1986	Church of God Oklahoma (John Tresscott) ⟶
1985		Church of God Denton Congregation (Austin Newell) ⟶
	1992	Sabbatarian Christian Fellowship (P. Frick & V. Lyle) ⟶
1988		United Biblical Church of God (C. Patton & C. Kimbrough) ⟶
1988		Church of God of Jessamine (Don Young) ⟶
1989		The Berean Church of God (Clarence Lucas)
1989		Evangelistic Church of Christ (G. Russel & C. Foland)
1990		Cornerstone Publications (James Rector) ⟶
1990		Alpha & Omega Christian Foundation (Grigore Sbarcea) ⟶
1990		Euclid Bible Publications (Gary Jordal)
1991		Family Church of God (Bill Young)
1992		Community Church of God (Thad Miller)
1992		Congregation of God Seventh Day Association (John Pinkston) ⟶
1992		Talent Ministries (Ted Phillips) ⟶
1993		Church of God Fellowship (Paul Bell) ⟶
1993		The Fellowship Church of God (Les Pope) ⟶
1995		Unity Christian Fellowship (Paul Haney) ⟶
1995		Christian Educational Ministries (Ron Dart & Larry Watkins) ⟶

1979 — Church of God Messengers (Gordon Weisler) ⟶
1979 — United Church of God (Richard Prince)
1979 — Christian Church of God (Neville Gilbert)

1979 — Biblical Church of God (Fred Coulter)
      1981 — Scriptural Church of God (Keith Hunt) ⟶
      1982 — Christian Biblical Church of God (Fred Coulter) ⟶

1980 — Christian Church of God (Jeff Booth) ⟶
1980 — Church of God New Mexico (John Shavers) ⟶
1980 — Church of the God Within (Tony Badillo) ⟶
1980 — The House of YAHWEH (Yisrael Hawkins)
1981 — Dallas Congregation of the Almighty (Herb Solinsky) ⟶
* — Church of God Kelowna (Hans Norel)
1983 — Transworld Publishing (Bernard Kelly) ⟶
1985 — Universal Church of God (Harold Hemenway) ⟶
1987 — Church of God Philadelphian Era (Martin Fillipello)
1987 — Triumph Prophetic Ministries (William Dankenbring) ⟶
      1995 — Patriots of the Kingdom (Myron Martin) ⟶

1989 — **Philadelphia Church of God (Gerald Flurry)** ⟶
      * — The Scattered Brethren (Lawrence Maayeh) ⟶
      1996 — (Dan Dawson) ⟶
      1996 — Church of the Philadelphia Elect (Colin Suttecliff) ⟶

1990 — Twentieth Century Church of God (C. Ken Rockwell)
1991 — Church of God of the Firstfruits (Frank Hassinger) ⟶
1991 — Church of God Philadelphia Era (David Fraser) ⟶

1991 — Church of the Great God (John Ritenbaugh) ⟶
      1993 — Church of God in Truth (J. Russell & D. Baker) ⟶

1991 — The Everlasting Church of God (Robert Collins)

1992 — **Global Church of God (Rod Meredith & Raymond McNair)** ⟶
      1994 — Church of God (Allen Cain) ⟶
      1994 — Pathway (Malcolm Crawford)

| 1995 | Friends of the Brethren (Norm Edwards) ➤ |
| 1996 | Church of God, Scriptural Organization (Wes Webster) ➤ |

1992	Bible Education Services (Don Hudgel) ➤
1992	Midnight Ministries (Malcolm Heap) ➤
1993	Reformed and Reorganized Worldwide Church of God (Don Gerlach)...............
1993	New Moon Seventh Day Church of God in the Netherlands (B. Otten & B. Rook) ➤
1994	Commonwealth Publishing (K. Gearhart & D. Conder)...............
1994	Christian Churches of God Australia (Wade Cox)...............
1995	The Plainer Truth (Bill Hillebrenner)...............
1995	Christ's Church of Grace (Earl Williams) ➤
1995	Worldwide Church of God Texas (G. Crow, W. Crow & H. Caudle) ───

1995	**United Church of God (David Hulme, Dennis Luker, Victor Kubik & Ray Wooten)** ➤
	1995	In Transition (John Robinson) ───
	1995	United Church of God, Birmingham (Ray Wooten) ➤
	1995	Orlando Church of God (Rob Elliott) ➤
	1995	Friends of the Sabbath (John Merritt) ➤
	1996	New Mexico Regional Church of God (Lon Lacev) ➤
	1996	International Biblical Learning Center (John Merritt & Don Ward) ➤

1995	Pinebelt Bible Association (Greg Taylor) ➤
1996	Barnabas Ministries (Alan Ruth) ➤
1996	Mystery Church of God (Ed & Cindy Burson) ➤

Key

Continues ──────➤

Discontinued ────

Unknown ....

* Date of origin unknown

Bold:
More than 3,000 members

18 Truths Restored by Herbert W. Armstrong

Armstrong's "18 Truths"	Kernel of Truth	Armstrong's Mistake
1) The government of God. When Christ comes, He will restore God's government to the whole earth. So you can be sure the one to come in the spirit and power of Elijah would restore God's government in his church. When Mr. and Mrs. Armstrong came among the Oregon Conference era of the Church of God (Seventh Day), the church had the right name, the law, the Sabbath and the tithing system. But they also had a government of men, with a biannual conference, voting just like they do in the world.	Wherever Christ is, the kingdom is present.	Jesus taught that John the Baptist fulfilled Malachi's prophecy (Matthew 11:14; 17:12). Herbert Armstrong identified himself as the fulfillment of Malachi's prophecy. Congregationalism is a legitimate form of church government.
2) The Gospel of the kingdom of God has been restored after 1,900 years. The Church of God (Seventh Day) did not have a clear understanding of the gospel; they emphasized what they called a "third angel's message."	The church should preach the gospel of the kingdom of God.	Herbert Armstrong believed the kingdom of God to be only in the future. He believed the message of the life, death and resurrection of Jesus to be a substitute, or false gospel.
3) The purpose of God, that we are to be born of God and become God. God is reproducing himself, and no other church on earth knows that or preaches it. As a counterfeit, they talk about being already born again.	God calls people to be his children.	There is only one God. Humans are not becoming God. "Born again" is a Bible teaching.
4) Who and what is God? God is neither one person or the Trinity. God is a family into which we may be born and also become God.	God is creating a spiritual family.	Testimony of Scripture is that God is one and reveals himself in three distinct personalities. As Matthew 28:19 teaches, we are baptized into the name of the Father, the Son and the Holy Spirit. Our heritage is not to become God, but rather, glorified children of God.
5) What is man? Do we have an immortal soul? Or are we just an animal? What happens at death? The dead are unconscious and they don't know anything. The Church of God (Seventh Day) people understood some of what happens at death, but not fully.	Man is not just an animal.	Whether deceased humans are unconscious or not until Christ returns is not of primary doctrinal importance. It is a mistake to allow a secondary issue to cause division.
6) The human spirit in man. What makes the difference between a human mind and an animal brain is that there is a human spirit with a human brain. That spirit is not the conscious part of the man. And it needs to be united with the Spirit of God.	God created humans superior to animals and salvation only extends to humanity.	Scripture speaks of the soul and the body (Matthew 10:28), as well as the spirit in man.
7) The church is only the firstfruits, and not the end of God's plan of salvation. God isn't trying to save the whole world yet. It starts with us, and we're being taught and trained so that we, under Christ, will be teachers and rulers when Christ comes to rule in the Millennium, when he starts to save the rest of the world.	The church is comprised of a harvest of the people of God.	Raising premillennial dispensationalism to the level of primary doctrine causes division in the body of Christ.
8) The church is not yet the kingdom of God, but we are the embryo that will become the kingdom of God. The WCG is the one and only true church!	The church is not yet all that it will be.	The Bible does not call the church an embryo. The saints are already in the kingdom (Colossians 1:13). There is no one corporate organization on earth that is "the one and only true church."
9) Only those whom God the Father calls and draws to him can be converted now. No other church knows that or believes it. Only those God chooses and calls now can come in and become part of the firstfruits. Satan has deceived the whole world, and the church is called out of that world.	John 6:44: "No one can come to me unless the Father who sent me draws him."	All Christian churches teach John 6:44. It was an error to teach that the WCG was the "one and only true church of God" and anyone outside the WCG was part of the "world" and therefore deceived.

10) The resurrection to judgment, the Great White Throne Judgment. God has a plan to save those who have not had an opportunity for salvation and who are now dead in their graves. They have not had the Holy Spirit. Their time is coming. But our time comes first, and we have to fight the devil, and they won't. In the Judgment, they'll be found guilty and condemned to death. They'll have their first chance to know that Christ came and paid the death penalty for them. They'll be allowed to accept that payment, and they'll have 100 years to prove they want to live differently than they did in their first life.	Everyone will stand before the judgment seat of God.	Several evangelicals believe that those who did not hear the gospel in this life will be confronted with it at the final judgment, and those appointed for salvation will believe and accept Jesus as Savior and Lord. Herbert Armstrong assumed such people would need another lifetime to "prove" faith by obedience. The mention of "100 years" comes from Isaiah 65:20, which Mr. Armstrong connected with Revelation 20:5, 11-12 as descriptive of a second physical life for humans who never heard the gospel in their first life. There is no proof that these verses should be connected.
11) The Millennium. The kingdom of God will rule nations on earth, and Christ and the saints will rule and bring prosperity to the entire earth. The Church of God (Seventh Day) understood the time duration, but, because they did not adequately grasp the full meaning of the gospel of the kingdom of God, they knew little in the 1930s of what the Millennium would be like.	Revelation 20 speaks of a 1,000-year reign of the saints with Jesus.	By equating the millennial reign of the saints with the kingdom of God, Herbert Armstrong's gospel became a message focusing only on the future. Neither Jesus nor the apostles preached a "millennial gospel."
12) The Holy Spirit coming into us only begets us. It opens our minds so we can understand the coded book, the Bible. Eye has not seen nor ear heard the things God has in store for us, described briefly in the Bible. God does reveal them to his church by his Spirit that resides in us. Without that Spirit, we cannot understand the Bible.	The Holy Spirit opens our minds so we can understand the truth of God in the Bible.	This truth has been part of Christianity for centuries. It did not need to be "restored" by the "end-time Elijah."
13) We are only begotten now, not born again. We are heirs, not yet inheritors. The Holy Spirit begets us as children of God, but we are not yet born.	The Holy Spirit begets us as children of God and Christians are to grow. Christians will be glorified and made immortal at the resurrection (1 Corinthians 15:52-54; 1 John 3:2).	Herbert Armstrong misunderstood the English translation as well as the Greek original. The Bible describes Christians as children of God, already born again (1 Peter 1:3, 23; James 1:18).
14) The identity of modern Israel. What are America's roots, our national identity? We are Manasseh, one of the lost 10 tribes of Israel. Numerous other groups have some knowledge of this truth, but no major denomination does. The Church of God (Seventh Day) officially rejected this truth.	America owes its blessings to God.	There is no proof in either the Bible or history that Americans are descendants of the northern 10 tribes of Israel. The New Testament witness is that all 12 tribes of Israel were represented in Judea and usually referred to collectively as "Jews" (Matthew 10:6; Acts 4:10; 5:21; 13:24; 26:7).
15) Prophecy can be understood only if you know that we are Israelites, and what prophecies apply to us and which do not.	Many prophecies applied to the people of Israel.	Anglo-Israelism leads to misunderstanding the Bible.
16) The annual festivals, the feast days. What other church knows about them or keeps them? Where did you hear it from? God revealed it to Mr. Armstrong.	The old covenant festivals served as shadows of Jesus Christ (Colossians 2:16-17).	The annual festivals were commanded for ancient Israel. God did not command anyone else to keep them, either before or after the crucifixion of Jesus Christ (Hebrews 8:13).
17) The authority of the sacred calendar, preserved by the Jews. Before Mr. Armstrong revealed this to the Church of God (Seventh Day), they were confused as to when the year should begin.	The Jews calculate the Jewish calendar and the dates of the annual Jewish festivals.	The Jewish calendar has no authority over Christians because the old covenant is obsolete (Hebrews 8:13).
18) Second and third tithe. What other church knows these points? The second tithe is for God's feast days. Other churches do not keep the feasts, so they have no reason to have second tithe. Third tithe is for the needy, primarily within God's church.	The New Testament teaches sacrificial generosity (Luke 12:33-34; 2 Corinthians 8:1-9,12; 1 Corinthians 9:3-15). Tithing is an appropriate form of worship, devotion and stewardship.	Commands for the second and third tithe are found only in Deuteronomy. They were part of a covenant now declared obsolete (Hebrews 8:13).

Doctrinal Comparisons

	Philadelphia Church of God *(Gerald Flurry)*	Global Church of God *(Roderick Meredith)*	United Church of God *(David Hulme)*
Church Government	Episcopal Form of Government Formed in 1989 and is a snapshot of the WCG in the 1950s. Many would describe it as a militant church of God. • "The Philadelphia Church is the ONLY PLACE ON EARTH where the GOVERNMENT OF GOD is administered, so says Mr. Armstrong!" *(God's Family Government*, p. 35) • "Recently Mr. Rod Meredith, who was considered the third man in charge of WCG for years, started his own church and now teaches COLLEGIAL GOVERNMENT. THAT IS THE STRANGEST AND MOST ABOMINABLE DOCTRINE OF ALL!" *(God's Family Government*, p. 27)	Presbyterian Form of Government Formed in 1992 and is a snapshot of the WCG in the 1960s. Many would describe it as the authoritarian church of God because of the number of known authoritarian pastors. • "Even after several years of guiding the college, Mr. Armstrong still did not clearly understand church government, and said so openly a number of times." *(When Should You Follow Church Government?* p. 5) • "All our members know that we have continued to practice the **same form of church government that Mr. Armstrong did!**" *(When Should You Follow Church Government?* **p. 37)**	A Mixture of Congregationally Representative and Presbyterian Form of Government Formed in 1995 and is a snapshot of the WCG in the 1970s. Many would describe it as the liberal church of God because it mirrors that period of time, known to insiders as the liberal years. • "In May 1995, the values of association for the individual churches in the United States was not something that was clarified. Indeed I would go as far as to say that an international association with rules of association for its own domestic region made little sense. It may in fact contain an inherent **contradiction.**" *(New Beginnings,* September 16, 1996)
Commission to the Church	• "God commands us to hear His word and WARN Israel. IT IS NOT A TIME TO RESTORE ALL THINGS AND/OR PREACH THE GOSPEL AROUND THE WORLD." *(The Ezekiel Watchman,* p. 9) • "Isaiah 22:20-25 means God used that man [Herbert W. Armstrong] and that man ONLY TO TEACH US ABOUT THE TRUE FAMILY GOVERNMENT OF GOD IN THE END TIME!" *(God's Family Government,* p. 4) • "As the end-time 'Elijah', Herbert Armstrong fulfilled Matthew 17:11 by restoring at least 18 points of truth to the era he was used to raise up." *(The Philadelphia Trumpet,* November 1992, p. 22)	• "The Global Church of God believes that the U.S., Britain, Canada, Australia, New Zealand, and democracies of northwest Europe are, in truth, the physical descendants of the 'Lost Ten Tribes of Israel....' Though some people may not like the trumpet blast of God's powerful warning message, it must be given if we are to remain faithful to our God's commission. God says to you and me, 'So you, son of man: I have made you a watchman over the house of Israel....' This inspired Ezekiel commission given to us is a wonderful and awesome responsibility." *(Global Church News,* November/December 1995, pp. 11-15) • "This is not the time when God is trying to save the world and the church doesn't exist to get as many people saved now as possible." *(Global Church News,* May/June 1994, p. 18)	• "Most branches of professing Christians assume that God intended for everyone to hear the message of salvation starting immediately after Jesus Christ's resurrection." *(The Good News,* May 1996) • "God the Father calls whom He chooses and leads them to submit to Jesus Christ. Those individuals who accept that calling and who receive the Holy Spirit comprise the Church of God. God the Father has made known to the Church, His family through Jesus Christ, His intention and purpose for the creation." • "The mission of the Church of God is to preach the Gospel of Jesus Christ and the Kingdom of God in all the world, make disciples in all nations and care for his disciples." *(Constitution of the United Church of God, an International Association)*
Gospel	• "Now the WCG teaches that Christ is the central figure of the gospel. That is tragically unbiblical." *(Malachi's Message,* p. 51) • "The Gospel is the good news of the coming Kingdom of God. The WCG talks about the gospel of salvation, the gospel of grace, the gospel of reconciliation, etc., etc. These doctrines are only part of the Gospel—not one of them is the true Gospel." *(The Ezekiel Watchman)* • "Mr. Armstrong was commissioned by God to preach the Gospel around the world. That was the first time the Gospel had been preached around the world since the first century! No one can logically deny that Mr. Armstrong did that." *(God's Family Government,* p. 12)	• "Some modern paraphrases render this phrase as 'gospel about Jesus Christ.' But this is a terrible mistranslation! The gospel is not a message about the Messenger; it is a message of the Messenger—His message, the message He was given to preach." *(Do You Believe the True Gospel?* p. 6) • "The gospel which Jesus had sent the apostles to preach was not centered on believing on Christ's person or receiving forgiveness of sins through His sacrifice." *(Do You Believe the True Gospel?* p. 9) • "Jesus NEVER said, please accept me or won't you give me your heart." *(The World Ahead,* September 1994)	• "Salvation through Jesus' life, death and resurrection is indeed part of the gospel message, but it is not exclusively (as many assume) the gospel message." *(The Good News,* January 1996, p. 35) • "Churches do not agree on either what the gospel is, or what the Kingdom of God is." *(The Gospel of the Kingdom - Web site)*

	Philadelphia Church of God *(Gerald Flurry)*	Global Church of God *(Roderick Meredith)*	United Church of God *(David Hulme)*
Nature of God	Believe in a form of polytheism (ditheism) holding that there are two separate Gods. Notice the following quotes: ● "But we will BE GOD—PART OF HIS VERY FAMILY!" (*WCG Doctrinal Changes and the Tragic Results*, p. 60) ● "No doctrine is more Satanic than the Trinity doctrine." (*WCG Doctrinal Changes and the Tragic Results*, p. 63) ● "The Holy Spirit is a power or force to convert us and bring us into God's family. The Bible rejects any idea of a third being." (*WCG Doctrinal Changes and the Tragic Results*, pp. 60-64) ● "Satan is intent on being on the same level with God and Christ. He is the third being of the Trinity. The Trinity doctrine is a direct reflection of Satan's desire to be God." (*The Philadelphia Trumpet*, November 1992, p. 7)	Believe in a form of polytheism (ditheism) holding that there are two separate Gods. Notice the following quotes: ● "But the Bible does not even once say that either the Father or the Son are omnipresent. Rather, as we saw in a previous article in this series, the Father lives in heaven, while the Son lived on this earth for about 33½ years. They weren't in both places at the same time. It is the Holy Spirit that is OMNIPRESENT—not the persons known as Father and Son." (*The World Ahead*, September 1994) ● "Some professing Christians believe 'God has a family,' but stoutly deny that 'GOD IS A FAMILY!' The proponents of the Trinity doctrine would have you believe that the God family is forever limited to only three divine Persons." (*The God You Can Know*, p. 27)	Believe in a form of polytheism (ditheism) holding that there are two separate Gods. Notice the following quotes: ● "The Holy Spirit is the mind and love of God in action in our lives. But nowhere does the New Testament teach that the Holy Spirit is a 'person' in the way that it teaches that God is our Father and Jesus Christ is His son." (*New Beginnings*, June 16, 1995) ● "The Holy Spirit, rather than being a distinct person, is spoken of in the Bible as being God's divine power." (*The Good News*, May 1996) ● "The Trinity is not part of God's revelation to humankind." (*The Good News*, May 1996)
Redemption & Salvation	● "God is reproducing Himself and no other church on earth knows that or preaches that.... God is a family into which we may be born and also become God." (*WCG Doctrinal Changes and the Tragic Results*, pp. 60-64) ● "One who is born of God is in reality, only conceived. Spiritual birth will only occur at Christ's second coming. So far, Christ is the only one to receive salvation." (*What Do You Mean Born Again?*) ● "God says, faith alone is dead or that salvation by faith alone is dead! Of course salvation can't be obtained by works. But you don't even become a candidate without works! Salvation is by grace—a gift. But without proper Sabbath keeping you'll never be saved!" (*WCG Doctrinal Changes and the Tragic Results*, p. 50) ● "We cannot earn salvation, but we must still qualify for it by overcoming." (*The Philadelphia Trumpet*, July 1992, p. 17)	● "The Bible reveals that the process of salvation is the means by which God the Father and Christ are reproducing their own divine kind." (*The World Ahead*, November 1993) ● "In plain language, God was indicating that They—the God Family now known as the Father and His Son Jesus Christ—would begin to reproduce themselves—to add more members to the God Family!" (*Your Ultimate Destiny*, p. 10) ● "Using a human analogy, we are now 'begotten' children of God, still in our Mother's womb, but growing in grace and knowledge so that we may be Born of God at the resurrection." (*Your Ultimate Destiny*, p. 19) ● "How can you be filled with ALL the 'fullness of God' and not be God?" (*Your Ultimate Destiny*, p. 31)	● "God wants you to be like Him in every way as His son or daughter so that you will be part of His very family at the time of the resurrection." (*The Good News*, May 1996) ● Salvation is received by taking many necessary steps. "Baptism and related steps we must take are only the beginning of the road to eternal life. Before we arrive at our ultimate destination, however, there are miles of road to travel." (*The Road to Eternal Life*) ● "We believe God's purpose for mankind is to prepare those whom He calls, and who elect through a life of overcoming sin, developing righteous character, and growing in grace and knowledge, to possess the kingdom and to become Kings and priests reigning with Christ on His earth after his return. We believe that the reason for mankind's existence is literally to be born as spirit beings into the family of God." (*Fundamental Beliefs*)

	Philadelphia Church of God *(Gerald Flurry)*	Global Church of God *(Roderick Meredith)*	United Church of God *(David Hulme)*
Legalism	Believe that Saturday is the only correct day of worship and the seven Holy Days given to ancient Israel are commanded observations under the new covenant and that it is a sin not to observe them. Therefore, these days are required for salvation. Notice the following quotes: ● "Listen to God's end-time prophet, Gerald Flurry: 'God began to reveal Malachi's Message to me.... Some people scoff at this, but it is still true and shall be true forever!'" *(The Philadelphia Trumpet, October 1996, p. 11)* ● "The Sabbath day was created for man so we could learn how to be God! This is the essence of the Gospel." *(The Philadelphia Trumpet, August 1992, pp. 20-21)* ● "God's faithful elect must never forget that HWA said, 'How subtly Satan used makeup to start the Church off the track.'" *(WCG Doctrinal Changes the and Tragic Results, p. 19)* ● "This is how you 'deliver thy soul' or save your life! IT'S YOUR TICKET TO A PLACE OF SAFETY! If you don't warn the WCG and Israel, YOU PAY WITH YOUR BLOOD!" *(The Ezekiel Watchman, p. 10)* ● **"We have not changed, or even tampered with, even one of Mr. Armstrong's 18 restored truths.** Mr. Meredith's group started in early 1993 and already has attempted to destroy the most important truth of those 18 restored truths—government!" *(God's Family Government, p. 52)*	Believe that Saturday is the only correct day of worship and the seven Holy Days given to ancient Israel are commanded observations under the new covenant and that it is a sin not to observe them. Therefore, these days are required for salvation. Notice the following quotes: ● "Satan has substituted his day (Sunday, the day of the sun) in place of the Seventh-day Sabbath." *(Global Church News)* ● "So the Sabbath is a test commandment—the one that really shows who is committed to God's way." *(The World Ahead, September 1995, p. 13)* ● "2 Corinthians 3:6-11—But this is where many go astray. They assume that the stones on which the administration of death was written were the stone tablets Moses received from God.... Paul was not talking about stone tablets. He was talking about massive stone walls." *(The World Ahead, May 1995)* ● "It should be comforting to know that the major Christian denominations throughout history have not been demonstrating God's plan for this world." *(What Is a True Christian? p. 5)* ● **"Incorporated in our Constitution and Bylaws is a statement saying, 'all major doctrines are those in the Worldwide Church of God at the death of Mr. Herbert W. Armstrong on January 16, 1986.'"** *(Global Church News)*	Believe that Saturday is the only correct day of worship and the seven Holy Days given to ancient Israel are commanded observations under the new covenant and that it is a sin not to observe them. Therefore, these days are required for salvation. Notice the following quotes: ● "The Sabbath is also a test commandment demonstrating our level of commitment to obeying God regardless of any consequences. The Sabbath also lays the groundwork for our relationship with God and the religion of the heart." *(The Good News, January 1996)* ● "Christ has not become our Sabbath rest, thereby negating the need for Sabbath observance." *(New Beginnings, September 16, 1996, p. 10)* ● "We believe that those meats that are designated 'unclean' by God in Leviticus 11 and Deuteronomy 14, are not to be eaten." *(Fundamental Beliefs)* ● "Who but those who understand the meaning of those Holy Days truly comprehends the vastness of God's mercy? Can you find any other faith that understands the breadth of God's compassion?" *(New Beginnings, September 16, 1996, p. 10)* ● "Mr. Armstrong's 18-point list of restored truths, while not a doctrinal statement in itself, stands confirmed in its essentials by the board." *(New Beginnings, June 16, 1995)*

Worldwide Church of God
Statement of Beliefs

We believe:

...in one God, who, by the testimony of Scripture, is one divine Being in three eternal, co-essential, yet distinct Persons–Father, Son, and Holy Spirit.

...that Jesus is the Son of God, by whom and for whom God created all things. As God manifest in the flesh for our salvation, he was begotten of the Holy Spirit and born of the virgin Mary. Jesus is the Lord of all, worthy of honor and reverence. As the prophesied Savior of humanity, he died for our sins, was buried, raised from the dead, and ascended to heaven, where he mediates between humanity and God. He will come again to reign as King of kings over all nations.

...that the Holy Spirit is the divine Comforter, promised by Jesus Christ and sent from God to the church on the Day of Pentecost. As the third Person of the Godhead, the Holy Spirit is God in us. The Holy Spirit transforms humans through repentance, baptism, sanctification, and continual renewal.

...that the Holy Scriptures, comprised of the Old and New Testaments, are the foundation of truth and the accurate and infallible record of God's revelation to humanity.

...that salvation is forgiveness and deliverance from the bondage of sin and death. It is the gift of God, by grace through faith in Jesus Christ, not earned by personal merit or good works.

...that repentance is the change of mind and attitude toward God that follows conviction by the Holy Spirit through the Word of God. Repentance entails a keen awareness of one's hopeless, sinful condition apart from the grace of God through faith in Jesus Christ.

...that the church is the collective body of all believers, regardless of denomination, who are called by God and in whom the Holy Spirit abides. The church began on the Day of Pentecost and was commissioned to preach the gospel, to teach everything that Christ commanded, to baptize, and to nurture the flock.

...that the gospel is the message preached by Jesus Christ and by the church about salvation through faith in Jesus and the reconciliation of humanity to God through Jesus as mediator. It is the good news of what God has done, is doing, and will do through Christ, and the central message of the Old and New Testaments.

Statement of Faith
National Association of Evangelicals

1. We believe the Bible to be the inspired, the only infallible, authoritative word of God.

2. We believe that there is one God, eternally existent in three persons: Father, Son, and Holy Spirit.

3. We believe in the deity of our Lord Jesus Christ, in his virgin birth, in his sinless life, in his miracles, in his vicarious and atoning death through his shed blood, in his bodily resurrection, in his ascension to the right hand of the Father, and in his personal return in power and glory.

4. We believe that for salvation of lost and sinful man, regeneration by the Holy Spirit is absolutely essential.

5. We believe in the present ministry of the Holy Spirit, by whose indwelling the Christian is enabled to live a godly life.

6. We believe in the resurrection of both the saved and the lost; they that are saved unto the resurrection of life and they that are lost unto the resurrection of damnation.

7. We believe in the spiritual unity of believers in our Lord Jesus Christ.

In May of 1997 the Worldwide Church of God was accepted as a member of the National Association of Evangelicals. The WCG endorses the NAE Statement of Faith.

WORLDWIDE
CHURCH OF GOD
·
Making a Difference for the Kingdom

Refer to our Web page at http://www.wcg.org